The Misfortunes of Prosperity

The Misfortunes of Prosperity
An Introduction to Modern Political Economy

Daniel Cohen

translated by Jacqueline Lindenfeld

The MIT Press
Cambridge, Massachusetts
London, England

This expanded and revised edition of the work originally published as *Les infortunes de la prospérité* (Julliard, 1994) is published with generous assistance from the French Ministry of Culture. Translation was supported by the Centre National du Livre.

Set in Sabon by Wellington Graphics.
Printed and bound in the United States of America.

Library of Congress Cataloging-in-Publication Data

Cohen, Daniel.
   [Infortunes de la prospérité. English]
   The misfortunes of prosperity : an introduction to modern
   political economy / Daniel Cohen : translated by Jacqueline
   Lindenfeld.
      p. cm.
   Includes bibliographical references and index.
   ISBN 0-262-03230-9 (alk. paper)
   1. France—Economic conditions—1945– 2. Economic
history—1945– 3. Keynesian economics. 4. Economics. I. Title.
HC276.2.C59813   1995
338.9—dc20   94-47022
                                                    CIP

Joseph said to Pharaoh, "Pharaoh's dreams are one and the same: God has thus foretold to Pharaoh what he is about to do. The seven healthy cows are seven years, and the seven healthy ears are seven years; it is the same dream. The seven lean and ugly cows that followed are seven years also, as are the seven empty ears scorched by the east wind; they are seven years of famine."
—Genesis 41: 25–27.

Contents

Introduction

The end of a decade, the end of a century, the end of a millennium—each of these perspectives sheds a different light on the political economy of our time.

Let us start with the millennium perspective. Only a couple of centuries ago, the societies of the world now known as industrialized nations initiated a process of transformation of their way of life for which the only valid parallel probably is the Neolithic period (when mankind invented agriculture). Throughout the nineteenth century the population was pushed to the cities, where it first encountered want, disease, ignorance, squalor, and idleness, the five scourges which the welfare state would try to eradicate in the twentieth century. At the time, it was not clear where this process would go: a combination of large miseries and large wealth? a short-lived process that would necessarily stop sooner or later? Few nineteenth-century economists bet that this process would last indefinitely, and even fewer thought that it would eradicate the poverty of the working class. From Thomas Malthus to John Stuart Mill, most economists writing in the first half of the nineteenth century thought that "growth" (to use an anachronism) would soon die out. The economy, it was believed, would reach a "stationary" state: an immobile world in which an equilibrium between cities and countryside would be reached, in which the work of those who die would be just balanced by the work of those who get born. It did not come out that way. Growth did last, and it did (mostly) eradicate the poverty of the workers, carrying along society as a whole in its march forward, mystifying all critiques and alternatives to the capitalist system. While this process blossomed, the view that wealth and miseries were to come together became progressively lost, especially during the years that followed the post-World War II period, and especially in Europe.

The thirty years that followed the war were so brilliant in Europe that the French economist Jean Fourastié called them the "thirty glorious years" (in reminiscence of the "three glorious days" that brought down the Bourbon monarchy). European growth averaged a healthy 5 percent a year, and it seemed to be granted forever. When it fell to about half this rate after the oil shock, European nations first could not believe that this fall would last; and all cried for the old rates. It took time before one would realize that it was the "thirty glorious years" which were exceptional, and that a 2–2.5 percent growth rate is perfectly in line with the twentieth-century average, and far above what was ever experienced before. The reason behind the postwar exception is not hard to find. Europe simply caught up to the United States during that time. Extrapolating Europe's postwar growth, as most Europeans wanted, was simply as gross a mistake as extrapolating China's current (10 percent a year) growth to the indefinite future, even beyond the time when it would get as rich as us. If European growth appears to be "too low" these days, it is not in reference with history, but only in reference to the expectations or the social institutions that were build up in the 1960s. And if Europe's unemployment is "too high," one should not blame it on growth, but rather on the set of expectations and institutions that were built up in the years of affluence. Will Europe have to abandon these institutions in order to fight its ever rising unemployment rate? Or is there a way out of unemployment within them? The question is obviously of interest to the United States at a time when that country is pondering the need to strengthen its own social institutions.

Although U.S. growth was lower than European growth by about half in the 1960s, there is no less nostalgia for those years in the U.S. The children of the 1960s could all hope to exceed their parents' standard of living within a short time. The children of the 1980s are now often satisfied with just being able to maintain a level of income equivalent to that of their parents. But it also appears that there has been a change not only in the level of economic growth, but also in its very nature. It is no longer a blazing trail which seems to bring affluence to anyone who makes the effort to embark on it. It is (almost) as destructive as it is creative and its course, while making society more affluent, also destabilizes it. Should we let go of our dream of a harmonious growth in which economic and social progress necessarily go hand in hand? Should we lament "the end of the Great American Job" (*Time* magazine), or are we the victims of an optical illusion which presently makes a cyclical crisis appear permanent but will soon disappear?

As these questions about the vulnerability of our societies build up, one could have expected an increased demand for state intervention. When societies become more unequal, should not it be the role of the state to intervene and sweeten the verdict of markets? It seems that the answer should be negative. The "conservative revolution" worshipped what the 1960s had burned: profit, monetary orthodoxy, individualism. Is such a shift a matter of decade-long political cycles? Will the

1990s look like the 1970s: years of disenchantment that will perhaps open the route to a new cycle? There are many reasons to think that this decade-long view is correct. Yet one cannot rule out a century-long story that may explain why the role of the state is doomed to be weaker in the twenty-first century than in the twentieth.

A century ago, the dominant view was still in favor of "laissez-faire" ("let it be"—without intervening). In the late nineteenth century, the Supreme Court of the United States was still pronouncing an income tax unconstitutional, and in most Western democracies government expenditures did not exceed 10 percent of national income (and most of it consisted of paying off debts for past wars or preparing for new ones). In part under the "rival" pressures of political models as different as Nazism or Bolshevism, democracies undertook radical transformations in the role of government in society. Today, European governments spend or redistribute close to 50 percent of total income (a figure which is lower in the United States because health care, which has now become a subject of hot debate). Squeezed by tight budget constraints and by the new global competition of poorer countries, the welfare state of the rich countries is under pressure. Are the new patterns of growth too low to sustain the welfare state? Can one claim that the globalization of the economy is about to impose on the twenty-first century a new laissez-faire model that would somehow take us back to the nineteenth century model? Such are the questions than one needs to address when contemplating the fate of the state in the coming century.

Is the millennarianist dream of affluence for all over? Has there been a disruption of the balance between the twentieth-century search for solidarity and the search for efficiency in our societies, to the detriment of solidarity? Is the political cycle of the 1980s about to end? These closely related issues constitute the subject of the present study. They will be addressed in order: Is the growth process about to enter a new phase (chapters 1 and 2)? Is the welfare state in crisis (chapters 3 and 4)? Is the political cycle (1960s versus 1980s) itself a standard one which is about to end (chapter 5)?

In attempting to address these questions, I have made extensive use of economic theory as it has developed over the last twenty years. Political economy, buried as it is in esoteric journals and hidden behind an increasingly mathematical language, is alive and well; its debates definitely center on the real world, and not on arcane topics as some people would like to think. The present work can serve as an introduction to contemporary political economy as well as a tribute to it.

Acknowledgements

This book could never have been written without the caring support of Anne Laporte, Michael Cohen, José Achache, and Michel Marian, or without the help of Perrine Simon-Nahum at Julliard and Ann Sochi at The MIT Press. To all, my heartfelt thanks.

The Misfortunes of Prosperity

1

Slowdown in Growth

In 1946 someone living in Duelle, a small French village located in Quercy, had to work 24 minutes to buy a kilogram of bread, 45 minutes for a kilogram of sugar, 7 hours for a kilogram of butter, and 8 hours for a one-kilogram chicken. Foodstuffs accounted for three-fourths of the total consumption, half of them being bread and potatoes. Butchered meat was purchased and consumed only once a week on the average. Butter was practically unknown. Clothing accounted for more than half of the remainder of personal consumption. Except for army duty, the great majority of people had traveled only on their honeymoons and on occasional pilgrimages.

Thirty years later, agricultural work was 12 times as productive in the same village. Only 85 minutes of working time was now needed to buy a kilogram of butter. In 1946 there were 208 people working in agriculture in Duelle out of a total population of 534; there were also 12 non-agricultural workers, 27 craftsmen, and 32 people employed in tertiary services. In 1975 the same village had only 53 people working in agriculture out of a total population of 670; there were 35 non-agricultural workers, 25 craftsmen, and 102 people working in services. In 1946 two infants under 12 months of age died every year; by 1975 the figure was one per two years. Twenty-year-olds were, on average, 1.65 meters tall in 1946; by 1975 the average height had gone up to 1.72 meters. New houses used to be built at the rate of 3 per 20 years; 50 were built in 1975. There used to be 5 automobiles in the village; there were 280 in 1975. The number of television sets had gone from two to 200, the number of washing machines from zero to 180, and the number of refrigerators from 5 to 210.

This particular instance, cited by Jean Fourastié in his book *Thirty Glorious Years,*[1] is illustrative of the changes that transformed France in the period between the end of World War II and the mid 1970s. "In 1946," writes Fourastié, "France had the occupational structure of a 'developing' country; farmers were not in the majority any longer, but they still represented over one third of the working population; by 1975 they represented but one tenth of it. It had taken 150 years for the proportion of the working population involved in agriculture to be reduced by half; in a span of 30 years that proportion went down from 36 to 10. Inversely industry gained 20 percent. But the tertiary sector came to constitute the majority, jumping 19 points in 30 years—in contrast with the 45 years, from 1900 to 1946, it had previously taken to go up 4 points!"[2] Two out of three employed women now worked in the tertiary sector. The same goes for the general evolution of the working population. In 1946, 51 out of every 100 French individuals were working; in 1975, only 41 were, and they provided much more wealth for the nation.

Modernity came to this French village like a bolt of lightning, as in so many other places in Europe and in Japan. In a few decades, all the remaining back yards of Europe vanished. At the risk of mild caricature, one can say of these remote part of Europe that they went from the pre-industrial era to modernity in 30 years.

Table 1.1
Growth rates of per-capita income (percent). Source: Angus Maddison, *Dynamic Forces in Capitalist Development* (Oxford University Press, 1991).

	1820–1989	1870–1989
Germany	1.6	2.0
England	1.7	1.8
France	1.5	1.8
Japan	1.9	2.7
United States	1.7	1.8
OECD average	1.6	1.9

Europe's growth rate over these glorious 30 years has averaged an outstanding 5 percent per year—far above the secular average of about 2 percent, and twice the U.S. average over the same period. When growth gradually decreased from 5 percent in the 1960s to 3 percent in the 1970s to about 2 percent in the 1980s, Europeans felt that it had simply abandoned them for no good reason. What they could not understand (and what they still often fail to understand) is that Europe was simply moving back to its secular average. Table 1.1 shows this unambiguously.

The irony is that growth in the vicinity of 2 percent per year would have been totally unthinkable to the economists who wrote in the early nineteenth century (and to some who wrote in the middle of that century). A growth rate of 2 percent per year means that per-capita income is multiplied by 7 over a century. This is an extraordinary figure in relation to the history of mankind. By way of comparison, historians are inclined to think that a Roman slave had just about as much as a seventeenth-century French peasant—which would indicate that per-capita income probably remained more or less constant over a millennium and a half. What was it that made for such a high growth rate (from a historical perspective) in this century, and should we fear that the twentieth century was an exception? Let us explore this question from the historical and theoretical perspectives before embarking on an analysis of the nature and cause of contemporary growth.

Modern Economic Growth in Perspective

For a long time, from the Neolithic period ("only" 12,000 years ago) to the eighteenth century of our era, mankind's main economic activities were to till the soil and to raise cattle.[3] Every millennium or so a major discovery would increase the productivity of peasants. The first major discovery was the invention of agriculture, which overthrew hunting and gathering as the way to feed oneself. In the tenth century of this era, farmers who used to fashion their own tools, most of them wooden and not very profitable, "suddenly" raised the efficiency of these tools by making most of them of iron, while turning to more efficient non-human sources of energy thanks to the horse collar and the water mill. Every time such a major discovery was made, the result appears to have been the same. Agricultural progress first allowed people to be better nourished, and the population grew as the death rate went down and the birth rate up. However, in a couple of centuries the progress of agricultural productivity was outstripped by the population growth that it had induced. An era that had started with a new abundance of food always ended with a famine. For example, the famines that started to hit Europe in the early fourteenth century were so harsh (especially in combination with the plagues) that, a century later, Europe's population was 40 percent lower.

This process explains why, despite repeated improvements in the methods of cultivating the Earth, standards of living remained essentially unchanged over the centuries: rising population, rather than rising per-capita income, was the mark of "progress."

All this changed with the "industrial revolution" of the last quarter of the eighteenth century. How this "industrial revolution" was actually started by a new "agricultural revolution" in the early eighteenth century is summarized in appendix A. In brief, the mechanisms at work were these: The progress of agriculture (due, this time, to the selection of seeds and the introduction of new crops) boosted the demand for metallurgy (as the new agricultural revolution raised the demand for iron tools) and increased the resources that farmers could spend on clothing. This pressure of "demand" induced major discoveries in textile production (Hargreaves's spinning jenny, Arkwright's water frame, and Crompton's mule are the key discoveries here), in the iron industry (the substitution of coke for charcoal in steelmaking), and eventually in the energy sector (to boost the productivity of the former sectors) with the development of Watt's steam engine.

Although the industrial revolution was clearly different in nature from the previous agricultural revolutions, the economists of the time did not believe that it would end up differently. From Ricardo to Malthus to John Stuart Mill (the "classical economists" who wrote in the first half of the nineteenth century), most economists thought that it would end up as before. Technological progress, they believed, would be a one-shot phenomenon that would soon be exhausted by the rising population. Land would sooner or later come to be too scarce relative to the population, and only famines could end—as they always had before—the unavoidable agricultural bottleneck.

It did not turn out that way. Technological progress kept raising the productivity of agriculture enough so that labor was continuously shed from the countryside to the cities, and the progress of trade helped the rich countries to import from abroad the food that they needed. Western Europe experienced its last famine in the 1840s.

For the authors who wrote in the second half of the nineteenth century, agricultural bottlenecks were no longer a matter of concern. To them, the key question was whether the march of capitalism would be stopped, not by lack of land, but by lack of capital. Both Marxists and neoclassical economists thought it would.

To Marx, for whom the only source of profits was the exploitation of the workers, the accumulation of capital had to stop sooner or later. If capital were to become too great relative to the number of workers, how would the capitalists get paid their profits? Although capitalists could try to make the working class poorer and poorer (at least relative to the wealth produced), there would necessarily come a point when too much capital per worker would force the profit rate to fall. Capitalism was bound to go into deep and repeated crises.

To the neo-classical economists (who updated the thinking of Ricardo and his followers), capital was subject to the same law of diminishing returns as land. When too many peasants work a given piece of land, the productivity of each of them has to fall. On a given plot, you cannot double the production of corn by simply doubling the number of peasants; land becomes too scarce. Similarly, when there were too many workers on a given stock of machines, their productivity would fall off. In contrast with land, however, the stock of capital can be raised to match a growing number of workers: demography is not a problem in a capitalist society. On the other hand, for a given worker, the number of machines cannot be raised indefinitely. One secretary with ten keyboards is not ten times as productive. At the margin, capital's productivity is lower than on average: the tenth unit of capital bought is less productive than the first. This is why this school of thought is also called Marginalism. As more and more units of capital are accumulated *per worker,* the benefits to capital accumulation have to fall. Thus, the accumulation of capital per worker has to stop one day. By a different reasoning, one reaches the same conclusion that Marx did: that capitalism must reach a "stationary state" in which the stock of capital in the hands of workers is at its limit—a state in which, by implication, per-capita income (rather than the number of heads, as in the pre-industrial era) stops rising.

Six Facts about Modern Economic Growth

Nicholas Kaldor[4] gives the following six-point summary of the major features of economic growth in the twentieth century[5]:

1. Output per worker shows continuing growth, with no tendency for a falling rate of growth of productivity.
2. Capital per worker shows continuing growth.
3. The rate of returns to capital is steady.
4. The ratio of capital to output is steady.
5. Labor and capital receive constant shares of total income.
6. Wide differences in rates of growth of productivity among countries are observed.

The first fact is the major feature of modern economic growth: output per worker shows continuing growth. The data calculated by Angus Maddison show that one hour of an American worker's labor is 11.6 times as productive in 1989 as it was in 1870. Never before has such an improvement in productivity been observed.

The second feature highlighted by Kaldor contradicts Marx's prediction: capital accumulation (in proportion of workers) appear to be growing indefinitely. Paul Bairoch estimates that the average amount of capital in the manufacturing industry at the end of the eighteenth century amounted to a few months' wages. Today the average amount of productive capital must be measured in terms of two or three years. In the United States, the average amount of capital stock per worker in 1989 was five times what it had been in 1890.

Facts 3–5 as listed by Kaldor show Marxism and Marginalism to have made erroneous predictions. Fact 3 contradicts Marx's prediction about the tendency of the rate of profit to fall as more and more capital is accumulated per worker. Fact 4, while more difficult to interpret in Marxist terms, certainly contradicts the Marginalist idea according to which indefinite accumulation of capital per capita exposes it to diminishing returns. Fact 5 contradicts Marx's idea that, in order to counter the tendency of the rate of profit to decline, the working class is driven into "relative" impoverishment (that is to say, its income must deteriorate in relation to the wealth produced).

Fact 6 is tougher to analyze, so I will postpone it.

In sum, Kaldor's list of facts shows that capitalism challenges both Marx's and the Marginalists' analyses: it is characterized by an enormous accumulation of capital that is not affected by any of the laws (predicted by Marxism or Marginalism) of the tendency of the rate of profit or of workers' income to decline.

Solow's Neo-Marginalism

Robert Solow's theory,[6] published in 1956, allowed Marginalism (and Marxism, up to a few differences in language) to appear coherent again in regard to Kaldor's first five facts. As we shall see later, it was in reference to the sixth fact that Solow's theory (in its naive version) came to be criticized.

In order to account for the seemingly never-ending growth process, Solow added a third factor of production, namely "technological progress," to the two (capital and labor) that had been analyzed by Marxist and Marginalist theories.

In order to simplify the presentation of Solow's theory, let me just say that technological progress acts as an "enlarger" of the number of hours worked. The labor of 4 hours in the nineteenth century can be done in only 1 hour in the twentieth century. "Technology" is the hidden factor that makes for such higher productivity of labor. Because of the advance of science and its derivative, whose use is available to everyone, workers can use their time in a way that, so to speak, make them more efficient. With the same number of hours, not only can a secretary type a book, as she would have done 20 years ago; nowadays she can almost publish it. It is not that more expensive material is needed; it is simply that the technology of word processing makes the use of the secretary's time more efficient. In brief, technology works in a way that makes the "effective" population (in terms of productivity) higher than the actual (observable) population. Once this adjustment has been appropriately made, the paradox of never-ending capital accumulation per capita vanishes: relative to the number of "effective" heads, capital accumulation is not rising. One can accumulate capital to an extent equivalent to the growth rate of the *effective* population without having to fear the law of diminishing returns. Both capital and per-capita income can then grow at a pace equal to the growth rate of technological progress.

This new theory makes it easy to account for Kaldor's first five facts. Per-capita income and capital can increase indefinitely at a pace corresponding to the growth of technological progress (facts 1 and 2); the rate of profit on capital is stable over time, given the fact that the law of diminishing returns does not apply if the "effective" population increases at the same pace as capital. The same applies to fact 4. Fact 5 also follows from Solow's model. Every worker's income increases at the same pace as technological progress, which itself controls the rate of growth of aggregate output. It is therefore natural for the fraction of the value added that goes to labor's remuneration to remain constant.

Taking technological progress into account therefore makes it much easier for Marginalist theory to resolve the paradox of an endless accumulation of capital. One might say that it is "finally" explained: Solow's article was published in 1956, almost 100 years after Mill reaffirmed Ricardo's idea that indefinite growth is impossible. It should be noted that Solow's analysis gives only a secondary role to capital accumulation: in his theory capital "follows" technological progress. Capital accumulation is not the trigger for gaining wealth. Indeed the increase in effective population is what creates a demand for capital (just as the demand for capital is induced by population growth in "naive" Marginalism). This makes it clear why the working class need not get poorer for indefinite accumulation of capital to be sustainable. There is no doubt that the main "surprise" to Marxism, even more so than the capacity for infinite accumulation of capital (within a capitalist society), is this fact that the working class did not get poorer, either in absolute or in relative terms. Not only has capitalism survived an endless accumulation of capital; it also has been able to do so without having to make its workers poorer. As long as wealth comes from the increase of a technical progress that raises the ability of labor to use a given stock of machines, it is easy to explain how workers get their share of the growing wealth (as we saw with Kaldor's fact 5).

Accumulating capital more rapidly than the growth of effective labor, on the other hand, would be exposed to the law of diminishing returns and would soon be self-defeating. In this respect Solow's theory maintains the pessimism of Marxism and Marginalism: capital accumulation cannot do anything without that "other" factor named technological progress. Yet this pessimism regarding a nation's capacity for autonomous growth (beyond the increases in technological progress) turns into a reason for optimism as soon as one touches another issue, namely the poor nations catching up with rich nations. Let us keep in mind that in Solow's theory "technological progress" is really a "public good" to which everyone has access. Thus, a country is poor either because it does not save enough or because it stands at a less advanced stage in its process of capital accumulation (but not because it lacks technology). Let us examine this second hypothesis. Suppose that a rich nation and a poor nation both save 20 percent of their income. The volume of saving (at an identical rate) is of course lower in the poor nation, but, thanks to the law of diminishing returns, that nation can count on better productivity for its capital. For that reason, it will have a higher rate of growth, and thus in the long run it will "converge" toward the rich nation.

Technological progress therefore is a huge machine that produces wealth for everyone; it is the universal emancipator at the source of the wealth of the Western world. But why just the Western world (and Japan)? Why has it not helped the poor nations as well? This fundamental question led to a critique of Solow's theory. Before I get to that critique, let me first show how Solow's model can account for the tremendous growth in the postwar years once it is interpreted as a process of shrinking of inequalities within OECD countries.

From the Thirty Glorious Years to the Crisis Years

The Thirty Glorious Years (to keep using Jean Fourastié's words) represent a golden age in Europe, a period of all sorts of discontinuities. Europe's transformation in those years may have been more extensive than the one that characterized the previous millennium.

As simplistic as Solow's model may appear, it enables us to give a satisfactory account of economic growth in OECD countries during the postwar years. Right after the war the United States enjoyed higher productivity than other OECD countries. Throughout the postwar years the United States experienced a level of productivity growth that differed only marginally from that country's prewar level: it was around 2.5 percent a year both over the period 1913–1950 and over the period 1950–1973. By contrast, European countries experienced much faster growth after World War II. France's productivity, for instance, grew at 1.9 percent a year between 1913 and 1950. It shoot up to an average growth rate of 5 percent a year in the period 1950–1973 (see table 1.2).

There is no doubt that the "catching up" phenomenon (which, as we saw earlier, was the counterpart to Solow's model) accounts to a considerable extent for the postwar economic growth of Europe and Japan. Likewise, the slowdown

Table 1.2
Productivity growth (GDP per man-hour; yearly averages in percent).
Source: Angus Maddison, *Dynamic Forces in Capitalist Development*
(Oxford University Press, 1991).

	1913–1950	1950–1973	1973–1987
Germany	1.0	5.9	2.6
England	1.7	3.2	1.9
France	1.9	5.0	3.2
Japan	1.8	7.6	3.5
United States	2.4	2.5	1.0

in growth that has been observed since the mid 1970s is due
in part to the weakening of this engine of growth. In 1950, a
French individual's income was worth less than 40 percent of
an American's income, according to Maddison's estimates. In
1973 the figure was 75 percent—in other words, the parity gap
was probably no longer statistically measurable. There have
been even more spectacular developments in the case of Japan.
In 1946 a Japanese individual's income was worth less than 25
percent of an American's income. In 1973 the figure was 65
percent. By 1989 it had gone up to 80 percent, which makes it
comparable to the figure for France. By extrapolation we can
say that a slowdown in growth now appears inevitable in
Japan. Validating this interpretation of the slowdown in growth
"à la Solow" immediately raises two issues.

First why was the oil crisis apparently responsible for trig-
gering the simultaneous slowdown in all Western economies?
This can be answered as follows: Regarding the slowdown, the
writing was probably on the wall before the oil crisis, possibly
as early as the second half of the 1960s. However, the hour of
truth was slow in coming because of a truly exceptional infla-

tionary situation from 1968 to 1973. In spite of decreasing profits (due to wage increases and a slowdown in productivity gains), companies thought that the problem could be ignored, thanks in part to abnormally low real rates of interest due to inflation.

Second, given the strong growth experienced by European countries and Japan through their imitation of the United States, how should we interpret American growth? One point worth mentioning here is that, even in the case of the United States, a catching-up phenomenon was probably still in effect in the early 1950s; production techniques designed in the first half of the century (known as Taylorism) were still to be generalized (as their extension was slowed down by the crisis of the 1930s). Postwar growth in the United States, therefore, was due in part to self-mimetism. Then the United States may also have benefited from the effect of its lead over the other countries: growth in European countries and Japan opened markets in which Americans were able to make use of their comparative advantages.

But one must keep in mind that the United States did not experience especially strong productivity growth during the postwar years. As table 1.2 clearly shows, the key problem of the United States has been a fall *below previous averages* of its productivity growth *after 1973*. This slowdown was already noticeable in the late 1960s, when it first became a matter of concern, and was to become specifically worrisome in the second half of the 1970s. As Maddison's analysis of the determinants of economic growth shows,[7] U.S. growth after 1973 can be entirely explained by the accumulation of capital and labor, with no explanatory power left to technical progress! During the same period, Europe did keep technical progress alive, albeit at half the previous rate. How can the United States have lost any sign of rising technical progress at the time when computers and communications are perhaps about to bring a new industrial revolution? How can it be, to use a formula coined by Solow himself, that one sees computers everywhere except in the statistics that measure technical progress? One may think that measurement errors are important: How can one properly account for the effect of word processors on the work of a secretary? How can one properly measure the benefits brought by the new quality of the printing and the ease of changing the text? Beyond these measurement errors, however, one cannot properly understand the productivity slowdown in the United States if one fails to take into account the role played by services. When limiting the analysis to manufacturing, indeed, one observes a slowdown of productivity growth from 3.3 percent in the 1960s to about 2 percent in the years 1973–1990. While significant, this slowdown is really not such a matter of concern. Over the years 1960–1990, the average growth of productivity in manufacturing exceeded 3 percent a year. Services, on the other hand, experienced an average productivity growth of only 0.9 percent a year. And as early as 1950 the service sector represented over half of the jobs in the United States, as compared to approximately one-third in France or Germany and one-fourth in Italy. I will return to this fundamental issue in the next chapter, where I will discuss the distinction between "good" and "bad jobs."

To summarize: Economic growth, I have argued, is a matter of accumulating two different sets of inputs. One set consists of material inputs—essentially labor and capital, which Marxism and early Marginalism thought of as the engines of growth. The other one is immaterial, consisting of the stock of knowledge (technological progress and organizational innovations) that a country can rely upon when merging labor and capital. When a poor country lags behind a rich one, it can use the stock of knowledge that the rich country has already accumulated to grow rapidly. On the other hand, it is the rich country's task to innovate and further the frontiers of knowledge; thus, that country's growth is bound to be slower and more erratic. From the latter perspective, Europe's and Japan's growth after the war are easy to interpret, and so is the slowdown that progressively took place, at least in Europe, during the 1970s. Obviously much more could be said about this interpretation of the slowdown of European growth. But if one accepts the view that Europe caught up to the United States during its "thirty glorious years," why is it that the other poor countries of the world did not do the same? Should we expect a catching-up phenomenon which, by the twenty-first century, would put all OECD countries in the same position vis-à-vis these countries that the United States was in vis-à-vis Europe during the 1950s and the 1960s? Should we expect a phenomenon similar to the one experienced in the OECD countries to occur on a world scale now? This fundamental issue forces us to reassess at least some parts of Solow's explanations.

A Critique of Solow's Model

We owe it to Solow to have taken classical and neoclassical political economy out of the impasse it had reached as a result of its consideration of capital accumulation as the sole engine of growth. Putting "technological progress" at the center of growth represented what must be regarded as a fundamental change of perspective—however trivial it may appear retrospectively. Technological progress implicitly is the gift of Nature, the philosopher's stone for which the economists were looking. Once it is applied to the human mind rather than to land or labor, technological progress can be said to result from this unique capacity of the human mind to produce more ideas than are needed to feed it.

How, then, is technological progress "accumulated"? The philosopher Alexandre Koyré used to say that Newtonian physics substituted its own mystery for the mystery of the universe. The same goes for Solow's "technological progress." It provides an explanation for the paradoxical aspects of growth (in relation to Marxist and neoclassical theories of growth); however, it does so at the price of pushing out of the economists' area of expertise what is now at the center of their theories. In relation to fact 6 as listed by Kaldor ("wide differences in rates of growth of productivity among countries are observed"), one is confronted with a "fact" that is none other than the mystery of inequalities between nations—a fact which Solow pushes out of the scope of his analysis!

If technological progress belongs to everyone, inequalities between nations should diminish. Let us empirically set the record straight by examining the overall performance of countries which have been developing since World War II and comparing it to the performance of rich countries (tables 1.3, 1.4). The data show no evidence of convergence of per-capita income between poor and rich countries. With the exception of Southeast Asia after World War II, not a single group of poor countries has experienced a higher growth rate of per-capita income than the group of rich countries. Solow's model thus fails to account for a major characteristic of the twentieth century: the persistence, or even expansion, of inequalities between nations.

Table 1.3
World economic growth in the twentieth century.

	Total income	Income per capita
OECD countries	2.9	2.1
Asia	3.2	1.3
Latin America	3.8	1.7
World average	3.0	1.7

Table 1.4
Growth rates of per-capita income (percent). Source: Angus Maddison, *The World Economy in the 20th Century* (OECD, 1989).

	1900–1950		1950–1987	
	Total income	Income per capita	Total income	Income per capita
OECD countries	2.2	1.3	3.9	3
Asia	1.4	0	5.5	3.1
Latin America	3.5	1.6	4.3	1.9
World average		1.1		2.5

The Theory of Endogenous Growth

On the surface it seems that it would not take much to let Solow's theory say that technological progress, rather than being a gift of (human) Nature, is a factor that accumulates as a result of investments (in research and development) which— just like patents or other types of investments—are motivated by the prospect of gain.

Here is where the problem would lie if such a theory of "endogenous" accumulation of technological progress were to be appended to Solow's theory. In Solow's theory, technological progress is a public good which does not figure in the distribution of value added between wages and profits. If instead we were to assume that technological progress should be paid, we would soon be faced again with the contradictions that appeared in Marx's or Marshall's analyses: the "rent" earned by inventors would soon hamper the remuneration of other factors of production (given the fact that technological progress is, in the long run, the only engine of growth). The "theory of endogenous growth" was developed precisely to deal with the dual constraint of having to make the growth of technological progress "endogenous" (that is, accountable in terms of economic reasoning) while retaining the implications of Solow's model for the distribution of income. Here, we are going along with the summary given by Paul Romer (co-founder with Robert Lucas of the theory of "endogenous growth") in his essay "Increasing returns and new developments in the theory of growth,"[8] which appeared in 1991. This new growth theory opens the way for fundamental revisions in the theory of growth, in terms of both its predictions regarding the level of growth itself and the nature of the processes involved. It will also enable us to tackle the correlational analysis of growth and employment in the next chapter.

A Return to Adam Smith

Romer starts by paying a tribute to Adam Smith[9] for his famous chapter on the division of labor. Smith explained in that opening chapter to *The Wealth of Nations* that the division of labor is the source of all productivity gains. In the famous instance of the pin factory, Adam Smith noted that 10 workers can produce 4800 pins a day, whereas the output of one worker left to his own devices would be 200 at the most. Centralizing the production of pins resulted in a twofold or threefold increase in each worker's productivity.

Smith regarded "the size of the market" as the limiting factor in this process. It might be an excellent idea to divide up tasks among workers, but one still has to find buyers for the output of 48,000 pins. If the demand amounts to 200 pins a day, the only possible solution is to use just one worker, even if it means lower productivity. However, as wealth increases, it is conceivable that the "endogenous" process of increasing productivity will start operating. One can then account for the possibility of indefinite growth in wealth: the richer a society gets, the more division of labor and increase in productivity take place, and the stronger growth becomes.

Adam Smith did not go that far himself. The instance of the pin factory led him to wish that the "market sphere" would be as broad as possible, and consequently he called for the liquidation of non-trading domestic activities and hoped that as many of them as possible would use the market as a conduit. In fact, at this particular stage in his work Smith was as much a philosopher as an economist; he wanted to prove that one should not be afraid to depend on others for one's survival, since one's subsistence corresponds to the interests of the individual on whom it is dependent. "Give me that which I want, and you shall have this which you want" was the motto Smith derived from the division of labor. "It is not from the benevolence of the butcher, the brewer, or the baker that we expect our dinner, but from their regard to their own interest."

Competition and Monopoly
For 180 years after the publication of *The Wealth of Nations*, economists turned away from the idea of increasing returns to scale—an expression that refers to the higher productivity of

tasks accomplished on a larger scale. They turned instead to the case that seemed the most natural to them: that of constant returns to scale (when you double all inputs, you simply double output). The reason for their choice lies in the work of Adam Smith himself. While stressing the beneficial effects of the division of labor, Smith also wanted to demonstrate that competition can bring about a "fair" and "effective" state of nature. This is the famous thesis of the "invisible hand" (the competition game) that leads one to "promote an end which was no part of his intention." Smith further says: "Nor is it always the worst for the society that it was no part of [his intentions]." This is reminiscent of a philosophical line that runs from Mandeville to Hegel.

However, economists were quick to realize that Smith's two propositions regarding the benefits of the division of labor and that regarding competition were contradictory. As demonstrated by the example of the pin factory, large firms have a competitive advantage over small ones: the economies of scale resulting from the division of labor enable them to sell at lower prices and drive the smaller firms out of business. As was also suggested by Marx (for totally different reasons), this argument leads one to forecast a greater and greater concentration of production, which sooner or later will necessarily be in contradiction with the idea of competition. Should all the manufacturing of pins (or bread) be concentrated in a single factory, the monopoly it would create for the owner might give him powers that would go against Smith's optimism regarding the market economy.

Schumpeterian Approaches
The problem disappears if one can conjure up what appears to be a contradiction in terms: monopolist competition. We owe

it to neo-Schumpeterian approaches to have revived this concept, which appeared in preliminary form before the war and then fell into oblivion with the success of Keynesian theory. The key point can be summarized as follows: Monopolies are short-lived. As soon as a firm attains monopoly power over some product, other firms will try to take it away by inventing products that will make obsolete the ones in the hands of the first monopoly. So rents are indeed paid to the inventors, but not for long. In Schumpeter's terms,[10] capitalism thus appears as a process of creative destruction, with the new things endlessly destroying the old ones.

In such a theory technological progress takes on a different garb. Far from being a gift of Nature, it becomes the result of a race toward ephemeral monopolies which will fall into companies' pockets. There is no longer a place for Solow's hypothesis that technological progress belongs to everyone, or for the conclusion that poor countries must necessarily "converge" toward rich countries. Indeed, in the neo-Schumpeterian theory I have sketched there are countless reasons for the competition between monopolies to be played out within the richest nations. Some of the reasons that make it impossible for poor countries to "converge" toward rich countries lie in education and in the mobility of research personnel from one firm to another within rich nations (the only ones that can pay for this manpower).

Is the Third World at an Impasse? (based on work by Paul Bairoch)

"Why is it that the industrial revolution, which originated in Great Britain, was gradually able to spread to approximately thirty rather different countries in Europe as well as America and Oceania, but could take hold in only one country which is not European or had not been settled by Europeans, namely Japan of course?" Paul Bairoch's historical analysis[11] presents evidence for the insights of the theory of endogenous growth. It provides an explanation both for the fact that European countries had no trouble catching up with the first industrial revolution and for the fact that the Third World has found it so difficult to catch up with the Second.

It was easy for the first industrial revolution (which began in the last third of the eighteenth century) to spread to European countries because the techniques involved were remarkably simple. Weaving machines and the first steam machines did not come as a shock to an eighteenth-century coppersmith. As Bertrand Russell emphasized, none of these machines were really scientific. Bairoch offers some examples of how easily European countries could copy English inventions. For example, simply by hiring a brother of the great English metallurgist Wilkinson, the French were able to reproduce an English steel factory. Around 1770 a "spinning Jenny" weaving machine was smuggled into France, and again a single element introduced mechanization to French industry. In 1823 Marc Séguin imported two English locomotives, which he set up in the middle of a workshop so that they could be scrupulously imitated (and only later improved upon).

By the time of the second industrial revolution (in the late nineteenth century), when electricity, automobiles, and chemicals led the chorus, technological mimetism was no longer possible. First of all, the capital intensity of the new techniques had changed drastically. The capital-intensity factor was low in the first stages of industrialization. Investment did not exceed 7 percent of GNP. Today a country must invest nearly 20 percent of its income to keep the capital-output ratio constant, and so poor countries need abundant savings (which their level of development does not always allow them to have). A vicious circle of underdevelopment thus builds up: poverty does not allow investment in either manpower or machines, and thus the original poverty is perpetuated. In addition to this quantitative obstacle, there is an educational one. In the early nineteenth century an illiterate ironsmith or coppersmith in a Western city did not face serious adaptation problems when shifting from his traditional workshop to one in which a few workers were involved in building relatively simple weaving machines or elementary steam machines. Today, a coppersmith in the Third World is overwhelmed by an electric locomotive or perhaps even by a diesel truck.

The Third World is thus confronted with an inversion of the sequence that led to industrialization in European countries. It can be said that in the nineteenth century education *followed* industrialization. In 1830 England's populace was 44 percent illiterate, and thus the percentage of illiteracy in the working class was between 60 and 70. In 1700 only one-third of the French population could read and write, and it was not until 1834 that the number of enlisted men who could write their names exceeded the number of those who could not. It was not until 1855 that women who signed their marriage certificates "X" became a minority.[12] Compulsory education came very late, almost a half century after the advent of the industrial revolution.

In the twentieth century, techniques created by the second industrial revolution required preliminary training which necessitated costly educational programs. And the greater the number of people, the more costly it is to try to educate them.

When the effects of the agricultural revolution of the eighteenth century started to be felt, the number of peasants was getting too high in Europe. Those who cultivated the lowest-quality land had to leave the countryside and go to the cities. The urban misery of the first half of the nineteenth century was the counterpart to productivity gains in agriculture which made a significant part of the population superfluous. In Fourastié's words: "The wretched then became the poor, that particular social class which Karl Marx had called the 'proletariat' and whose impoverishment he attributed to the beginning of capitalism—when in fact this social class was *created* by capitalism, by the gradual disappearance of famines and by new subsistence possibilities for those who earlier had not subsisted." In developing countries, on the other hand, demographic expansion preceded the industrial revolution; the medical revolution, imported from the West, came first, and agricultural transformation had to follow it (when it could do so). Demographic expansion has therefore exceeded the stockpiles of agricultural productivity, forcing poor countries to import the agricultural products they need and thus suffer from a savings deficit which has prevented them from getting involved in the spiral of continuous growth in wealth experienced by industrialized countries.

Although in the early nineteenth century the situation in the Third World was totally different from that in European countries, some countries managed to get out of the vicious circle of underdevelopment. The Asian "tigers" (Hong Kong, Singapore, Taiwan, and South Korea) are always used as examples, and rightly so. If the underdevelopment trap was unavoidable, how did they succeed in doing what other poor countries have failed to do?

Many arguments can be given to account for the success of the Newly Industrialized Countries (NICs). One of them is simply that their saving rates far exceeded those of other countries. While most countries in the world invest about 20 percent of their income, the "tigers" (with the exception of Hong Kong) typically invest 30 and sometimes 40 percent of their income in physical capital, and no less astounding numbers in education. By investing much more than the other countries, the "tigers" proved that it was possible to catch up to the rich countries by investing what it takes to be able to use the rich countries' knowledge.[13]

The other major reason why the Southeast Asian NICs could catch up to the rich countries is that, unlike other developing countries (in Africa or Latin America), they focused entirely on conquering markets in industrial countries. This strategy of extreme openness did not go without a certain amount of domestic protectionism, but it provided these countries with a capacity to import foreign goods which has turned out to be extremely beneficial. As Romer said, one does not need to reinvent the wheel if it can be imported. Such was the direction chosen by Southeast Asian countries when they opened up to markets in industrialized countries.

Other developing countries opted instead for "self-centered" development strategies, especially as a result of the traumas of the 1930s (when international trade collapsed). As a result of systematically protecting their producers from external competition, those countries had to "reinvent the wheel."

One can think of many other differences (some of them being of a political nature) which account for delays in development—one of the most significant in the case of Africa undoubtedly being the demographic trap. Nonetheless, the realization that "self-centered" development has misfired promises to have a tremendous impact on decision making in developing countries.

Few of the mechanisms capable of transferring technological progress (an ambiguous "public good") can be as effective as the trading of goods, as was proven by Southeast Asian countries in the 1970s and by European countries in the 1950s. From this point of view, the developing countries' chances of catching up to the rich countries are highly dependent upon their capacity to sell their goods to the rich countries.

Conclusion

Europe's growth during the 1950s and the 1960s may serve as an encouraging message that the developing countries can aim at rapid "transitional" growth of the same catching-up kind once experienced by European countries and Japan. Demographics and education (two phenomena which, as we saw earlier, are closely linked) stand in the way, but there is no reason to think that they are insurmountable. Opening one's economy and investing in human and physical capital is a difficult exercise, but it can be a rewarding strategy. Once this is done, the poor countries can use the stock of knowledge accumulated in the rich countries to grow rapidly.

In the rich countries, growth is much more dependent on the ability to innovate. In the theory of endogenous growth, innovation is a strategic variable that revives the course of "creative destruction" discussed by Schumpeter: it depends on the new frontiers of knowledge which are open by research and development, and it often comes at the cost of an endless destruction of past jobs and skills. Central to this new face of capitalism is its "old" form, the one that preceded the Thirty Glorious Years. Growth is now less smooth and more fragile, and it has lost the reassuring traits it had in the postwar period.

Paul Krugman has characterized the period that began in 1973 as "the age of diminished expectations."[14] Although the term was coined for the United States, it is perfectly adapted to Europe, where growth was never so large as during the 1950s and 1960s and where one can predict, at little risk of contradiction by the facts, that it will never again be so large for so long.

2

Jobs and Unemployment

Although the rich countries' disenchantment over growth was universal in the 1970s, slow growth did not yield the same response everywhere, especially regarding the working of the labor markets. In the countries belonging to the European Community, unemployment soared from below 2 percent in the 1960s to above 10 percent in the early 1990s. In the United States the unemployment rate exhibited no such trends, moving from 5 percent in the late 1960s to 6 percent in the early 1990s, but at the price of a quasi-stagnation of real (take-home) wages and at the further cost of rising inequalities. Either way, questions about the ability of economic growth to create "good" jobs flourished on both sides of the Atlantic. Beyond the nostalgia for higher growth one hears a more qualitative fear: something about the nature of growth, which would have changed, portraying technological progress as a factor of social destruction—causing job cutbacks rather than helping job creation, and causing rising inequalities rather than affluence for all. The same is said about trade, which is seen both as a growth opportunity and as a source of job destruction and whose balance, overall, might call for protectionism. It is this relationship between the qualitative nature of the growth process and the employment patterns that I now want to analyze. I shall first attempt to disentangle the correlation between technological progress and jobs before turning to the analysis of the labor markets on both sides of the Atlantic.

Machines and Unemployment

Does technological progress destroy jobs? As Alfred Sauvy put it, that would not be very surprising since such is its goal.[1] Aristotle had already characterized technological progress as serving only one function: abolishing slave labor. The whole history of technological progress is replete with fights by those who want to block it because it would "deprive the lower classes of their bread" (as the Roman emperor Diocletian put it in the third century of our era) and those who argue that (as Montesquieu wrote) "if windmills were not already in use, I would not think that they are as useful as is rumored, because they have idled an infinite number of hands."[2] A great many people whose inventions lifted up mankind's productive power had to face resistance from the trades and hands they were said to be idling. In 1744 Vaucanson's weaving machines were broken to pieces and he had to flee in disguise to save his own life. John Kay, the inventor of the "flying shuttle" (central to the development of the textile industry in the eighteenth century) also had to flee. Hargreaves, the inventor of the "spinning Jenny" and another founding father of the textile industry, found himself surrounded by angry workers who burned down his house and eventually caused him to die in misery. In the nineteenth century, silk weavers in Lyon turned their revolt against mechanization in the silk industry into political insurrection. In England the Luddites also proclaimed hatred for machines.

As Sauvy's examples illustrate, the fear that technological progress will eliminate jobs is nothing new. If a microchip or a computer can suddenly do the work of a million employees, a good number of them will inevitably be laid off. Society at large is made wealthier by the productivity gains that machines can achieve. At the same time, there is no doubt that, on the individual level, the employees that have been laid off are the losers—the victims of an innovation that brings wealth to the rest of society. Why does the rest of society not (always) succeed in offering them new jobs?

The first answer that comes to mind is that the rest of society finds itself in the same kind of precarious situation: If all sectors are governed by the law of technological progress, who will work and who will hire whom? In the first half of the nineteenth century, Sismonde de Sismondi warned against the danger of technological progress as follows: "Once workers are laid off, their consumption will decrease and consequently so will their demand. For this reason machines are harmful except if their introduction is preceded by an increase in revenue and, as a result, by new possibilities for the displaced workers."[3] The argument, as we shall see in the next chapter, anticipates Keynesian reasoning by a century. However, it leaves us perplexed. Suppose that all sectors are simultaneously affected by technological progress. Imagine that an inventor discovers a pill that enables all men and women to work twice as fast at their mechanical and intellectual tasks. Such technical progress simply means that there are now twice as many hours of working time. Would such an invention create unemployment? What would prevent individuals, if they were so inclined, from producing twice as many goods and becoming twice as rich? An indirect answer to this question is provided by Sismondi's claim that "as long as a nation can avail itself of a sufficiently large market to be assured of a prompt and profitable outlet for all its goods, each of these discoveries (the machines) is beneficial: instead of reducing the number of workers, it increases the work force and its output. . . . However, there comes a time when the civilized world constitutes a single market. Demand in this universal market is a precise quantity over which the various nations fight."[4] At the heart of the argument used by those who fear that technological progress will take jobs away is Sismondi's clearly expressed idea that, demand being limited, a reduction in the number of working hours must necessarily go hand in hand with productivity gains.

The idea that demand will never be able to keep up with the pace of productivity gains is the consumerist counterpart to the idea that growth in productivity gains must be halted. The idea of a saturation in the demand for goods, which is constantly contradicted by the reality, is erroneous at a general level even though it may be right in its details. If a radical innovation allows a tenfold reduction of manufacturing costs for a car, one cannot count on a proportional increase in the demand for cars; it will be prevented by the shortage of highways and parking lots and by the consumers' desire to spend money on other goods. On the other hand, it would be a totally different matter if there could be a general increase in productivity that would allow productivity increases proportional to the needs in all sectors related to automobiles (parking lots, highways, etc.) simultaneously with increased productivity for other consumer goods (textiles, televisions, etc.). It would allow an increase in the demand for all goods without the consumption of some goods being affected by the scarcity of other goods. But in the absence of such harmonious progression, one can see that the most productive sectors must suffer job cutbacks, while employment in the less productive sectors will expand, provided that the two types of commodities are not substitutable one for the other (in which case the more productive commodity would absorb the less productive one). We can therefore say that the need for a reallocation of jobs results from the (inevitable) asymmetric course of technological progress in various sectors, rather than from its overall progression.[5]

Uneven Technical Progress

The asymmetric course of technical progress over the last four decades can be roughly characterized as follows: Technological progress throughout the 1950s and the 1960s essentially affected industry, which caused a partial shift of employment to the service sector (which, generally speaking, has not experienced comparable productivity gains; see table 2.1 and the table in the appendix to this chapter for the sectoral data). The shift of jobs in the direction of services did not make the proportion of services in the aggregate volume of production go higher.[6] Employment really went in the direction of services to offset the lesser productivity of that sector: more jobs need to go to

Table 2.1
Productivity growth, 1960–1990 (yearly averages in percent). Source: *Labor Markets Trends* (OECD, 1990).

	Agriculture	Industry	Services
France	5.5	4.0	2.2
Germany	6.3	2.8	2.0
Japan	4.0	5.9	3.8
United Kingdom	4.9	2.8	1.6
United States	3.1	1.6	0.9

services in order to keep the output of services on a par with more productive manufacturing activities.[7]

When the transition to a service economy started, everyone welcomed the transition, as service jobs were initially better paid and less strenuous. Indeed, a productivity boom in manufacturing generates a higher demand for the service sector. As cars get cheaper, people want to go on vacations; the demand for hotels rise, and so do wages in that sector. As computers are introduced, the demand for software analysts rises; so do their wages. And so on. As time passes, however, more and more people move to these low-productivity sectors which perform tasks complementary to the high-productivity sectors (cars or computers, in the examples above). Downward pressures on wages start setting in. As more and more people move to low-productivity activities, the average productivity of the economy becomes more and more dependent on the ability of these sectors to grow. An age of diminished expectations begins. One extreme example: Assume that productivity in manufacturing becomes infinite. Manufactured goods can suddenly be supplied at zero cost, and they abound freely around the world. All of the working population moves to the service sector, where productivity has stayed bounded. One will then first engineer a one-shot increase in purchasing power (as the prices of manufactured goods go to zero); however, from that point on, income will evolve along with the slow growth of productivity in services. Any promises of future growth based upon the one-shot original gain would be deluded.

Beyond Services?
Today, however, technological progress affects the services themselves. In banks and insurance companies several thousand employees can suddenly be replaced by microchips. Conse-

quently, a large portion of the people who are currently employed in services will soon have to work somewhere else. Where can the jobless turn to find new jobs? This is a troubling question which one is sometimes tempted to answer by saying "nowhere"—hence the inevitability of unemployment, or at least of "poor" (badly paid) jobs.

Yet the general picture that has prevailed over the centuries should help. Jobs should be created where they are most needed: in the less productive sectors. Is there a chance that they will go back to industry? Indeed that might be feasible within the framework of a strategy of product-cycle acceleration, as exemplified by the Japanese experience: as services become more productive, a decrease in their cost can conceivably reorient the demand for labor in the direction of industry.

Where else can jobs go? The answer seems to be "to other services." Nurses, clerks, and teachers are in high demand. Productivity gains will probably be lower in these areas than in others. However, the crisis of the welfare state might stand in the way. In many of these sectors, the state plays a key role, especially in Europe. In the absence of a return to solvency in the areas covered by the welfare state, demand might be tied up in these particular sectors.

Is the economy condemned to lose jobs in the absence of a return to solvency in these areas? Theoretically there is no reason to think so. The contribution of the next weakest sectors (in terms of productivity) should do. However the difficulty to pinpoint clearly the sectors in which people could be hired is the sign of a real problem: increased uncertainty about job creation. It is difficult to assess the extent to which this is a new feature of capitalism. The workers who were driven into the cities from the countryside in the early nineteenth century as a result of gains in agricultural productivity are evidence of such a painful process. But this process certainly stands in sharp contrast with the postwar years, when the sectors that benefited from gains in industrial productivity were clearly identified (especially in Europe, where the United States could readily be copied): banking, health care, and education.

Job Creation and Job Destruction

Technological progress is not in itself a source of unemployment. If it were to come in "homogeneously" to society, it would simply allow every worker to produce and to consume more. In addition, if there is a positive growth of such homogeneous technological progress, there is a positive "capitalization effect" of growth upon employment. This point, emphasized by Christopher Pissarides,[8] is easily explained as follows: To the extent that the decision to hire a worker is really akin to an investment decision, faster growth will imply, *ceteris paribus,* a larger return on this investment, and the incentive to hire will be larger. Thus, a rise in the growth rate of technological progress should be expected to raise the demand for labor, not to reduce it.

On the other hand, the level of growth is not all; its nature counts as much. Imagine a perfectly still society in which the work of the fathers is done by the children when the fathers die (say, Japan in the seventeenth and eighteenth centuries). Such a society will experience zero growth and zero unemployment. Now assume instead that growth is brought on by a process of creative destruction in which old jobs are continually being destroyed and replaced by new ones; then there might be both rapid growth and a high unemployment rate. If more growth in reality means even more such transformations, it may mean more job destruction and perhaps more unemployment. Hence the schizophrenic nature of an attitude of resistance to

Table 2.2
Unemployment inflows and outflows.

		Monthly inflows[a]	Monthly outflows[b]	Long-term unemploy-ment[c]
European Union	1979	0.3	10.00	29.3
	1988	0.3	5.0	54.8
United States	1979	2.1	43.5	4.2
	1988	2.0	45.7	7.4
Japan	1979	0.3	19.1	16.5
	1988	0.4	17.2	20.6
Non-EEC Europe	1979	0.7	38.1	5.3
	1988	0.8	30.4	7.3

a. As percentage of employed people.
b. As percentage of unemployed people.
c. As percentage of total unemployment

technological progress accompanied by demands for stronger growth.

Obviously our societies are closer to the second model than to the first. As is evidenced by table 2.2, millions of jobs are destroyed every year in the OECD countries, and nearly as many are created. The table reports the percentage of people who move from having a job to being unemployed and the percentage of people who do the opposite and move from being unemployed to being employed. (In each case the number is given as a percentage of the population of origin.)

The first thing to be noted about table 2.2 is the extraordinary amount of activity in the labor market. In Europe, for instance, the yearly flow figures are approximately equal to the unemployment level. In the United States, they are four times as high! Taking a static view of unemployment is deceptive and fails to reveal the extent of the problem. A jobless individual is most often *between* two jobs, and this process of job creation and destruction shows the vitality of the economy as much as its fragility.

The next thing to be noted is that the figures are extraordinarily stable from one decade to another (apart from the two exceptions, which are underlined in the table). They show an increase in the number of the long-term jobless in the European Union (EU) and a correlative reduction by half of the percentage of jobless individuals who find jobs there. Other figures for unemployment inflows and outflows are remarkably stable. The United States clearly stands by itself: although the percentage of workers losing jobs is very high (2 percent per month), the percentage of jobless individuals finding jobs is also very high, and as a result the percentage of long-term unemployment is very low. It is also interesting to note that non-EU countries are not characterized by an inactive labor market, despite having only one-third the European Union's rate of unemployment. In those countries, relative to the EU countries, twice as many workers lose their jobs every year, but on the other hand six times as many jobless individuals find jobs every year. Accounting for European unemployment therefore means explaining why the jobless find it more difficult in Europe than in other places to get a new job, rather than explaining why more jobs are lost there (be it because of technological progress, international trade, or whatever).

Some Misconceptions Concerning European Unemployment
(based on work by Charles Bean)

This section is based on Charles Bean's brilliant article "European unemployment: A survey" (*Journal of Economic Litera-*

ture 32 (1994): 573–619). Let us first review some commonly heard clichés regarding European unemployment.

Unemployment as a Worldwide Phenomenon

The idea of unemployment as a worldwide phenomenon is a common feature of European rhetoric. "We've tried everything," French President François Mitterand once said, "but the crisis is all over the world, and there's nothing we can do about it. . . . " The data in table 2.3 clearly show, however, that unemployment is a European phenomenon and, even more specifically, a phenomenon unique to countries of the European Union. Neither Japan nor the United States nor any of the other

Table 2.3
Unemployment rates (percent).

	1966–1973	1974–1979	1980–1985	1986–1992
Belgium	2.7	6.0	12.2	8.9
Denmark	0.95	6.0	10.0	9.7
France	2.5	4.5	8.3	9.9
Germany	0.9	3.2	6.0	9.9
Netherlands	2.1	5.1	10.1	8.3
Italy	5.7	6.8	11.6	15.6
United Kingdom	3.4	5.0	10.5	8.9
United States	4.9	6.7	8.0	6.1
Japan	1.2	1.9	2.4	2.4
Austria	1.4	1.7	3.2	3.4
Finland	2.3	4.5	5.6	6.0
Norway	1.7	1.8	2.6	4.1
Sweden	2.2	2.9	2.8	2.4
Switzerland	0.01	1.2	1.9	2.3

European OECD countries (Austria, Switzerland, the Scandinavian countries except for Denmark) has experienced unemployment rates comparable to those of countries in the EU (when we limit the comparison to the 1970s and the 1980s). Table 2.3 summarizes the data for the most representative countries.

Failing to stress the specific nature of unemployment in the European Union can only result in misguided explanations. For example, anyone asserting that technological progress is the cause of unemployment would have to explain why it has had more of an impact within the EU than it has in neighboring countries. Likewise, any interpretation putting the blame on international trade would have to explain why it would take more of a toll in France than in such open countries as Switzerland and Sweden.

The Oil Crisis

The following analysis of unemployment in the 1970s used to be commonly accepted in the early 1980s. As a result of a rise in oil prices, some countries allowed wage cuts which enabled firms to maintain their solvency and hiring capacity. Meanwhile the refusal of other countries to do so, particularly in the European Community, resulted in continuously declining profitability for their firms throughout the 1970s, which eroded their hiring capacity.

The problem with this approach is that it does not account for unemployment in the 1990s. As early as the mid 1980s, profits were restored all over Europe, where unit costs kept decreasing under the joint effects of wage restraint and productivity gains. A few aggregate figures will suffice to illustrate. The loss of purchasing power resulting from the rise in oil prices was 3.3 percent for EU countries, 2.3 percent for other

European countries, 2.2 percent for the United States, and 6 percent for Japan. But productivity gains were approximately 2 percent every year! Therefore ,it is not surprising that all measures that proposed to deal with the wage disequilibrium caused by the oil crisis made it appear that it had totally vanished as early as the mid 1980s. In any case, in the second half of the 1980s the prices of raw materials returned to levels very favorable to the OECD countries.

It does not necessarily follow from these developments that the argument was based on false premises; rather, it has to be refined. It is possible, in particular, that firms reacted to the wage disequilibrium of the 1970s by making productivity investments which reduced labor costs and took effect at a time when lower wages would make those productivity investments less necessary. Substituting an intercom for a concierge (as became increasingly the norm in the 1980s) may have been rational planning, but its application might have come at a time when concierges would have worked for less, making the investment in their substitutes retrospectively inefficient.

Trade Unions

Should trade unions be blamed for having rigidified the economy and prevented job creation? After rising throughout the 1970s, the number of unionized workers leveled off for a while, then decreased slightly during the second half of the 1980s. Table 2.4 shows the aggregate picture.

As can be seen, the unionization "march" during the first half of the 1970s is a phenomenon peculiar to the EU countries and other European countries. However, unionization continued to make progress during the 1980s in European countries outside the EU, while it leveled off or decreased in the EU countries. Although "unionization density" is certainly a bad

Table 2.4
Unionization rates.

	1969–1973	1974–1979	1980–1985	1986–1990
European Union	37.7	42.0	43.4	42.6
United States	23.8	21.8	17.6	15.1
Japan	34.6	33.2	33.2	28.0
Other European countries	44.1	51.1	55.1	57.6

indicator of workers' aspirations to wage increases, table 2.4 does not in any way show the EU to be in either a particularly good or a particularly bad situation in this respect, as compared to other European countries. Therefore, the hypothesis that unemployment results from unionization is rather unconvincing—all the more so since England's unemployment figures were similar to those of other EU countries at the end of the 1980s in spite of what Bean calls the "emasculation" of trade unions.

Wage Rigidity in the Face of Unemployment
The other aspect of the union issue is the tendency of wages to decline as a result of unemployment, whether or not they initially caused it). In this respect, most empirical studies point to a significant difference between the EU countries and other European countries. The response of wages to unemployment is half as strong in the EU countries. One unemployment point brings wages down 1 percent in the EU, as compared to 2 percent in the rest of Europe. In Japan and Switzerland the figures are approximately seven times higher than they are in the EU countries. The United States, however, is in the same position as the EU countries. Contrary to common assump-

Table 2.5
Mandatory deductions.

	1969–1973	1974–1979	1980–1985	1986–1990
European Union	36.7	40.1	43.1	43.7
United States	29.1	29.8	31.0	31.8
Japan	22.2	24.6	29.6	32.9
Other European countries	41.7	46.2	49.1	50.8

tions, American salaries do not decline much in response to unemployment. However, in the United States unemployment disappears once the economic cycle becomes favorable again, whereas in the EU countries it always seems to stay at the level it had reached previously. Why? This is the fundamental issue to be addressed—an issue which the inelasticity of wages to unemployment cannot (directly) resolve.

The Cost of the Welfare State
Wages are not totally responsible for the rigidity of wage costs. In Europe over 40 percent of the labor cost is absorbed by social benefits. Net wages have remained constant since 1980 in spite of a cumulative increase in the labor costs (net of inflation). Gains have been totally absorbed by the welfare state. Table 2.5 gives the data for the OECD countries.

We can see that the increase in mandatory deductions is a phenomenon that only the United States has escaped (although in part at the cost of a heavy budget deficit). So it is definitely not a factor unique to the European Union. In any case, the welfare state cannot be in itself a source of unemployment. If (for any historical reason) the government were to be put in charge of centralizing expenditures for electronic games, no one

Table 2.6
Replacement rates of unemployed individuals' wages.

	1969–1973	1974–1979	1980–1985	1986–1990
European Union	51.8	53.4	57.7	57.4
United States	57.9	55.8	55.1	54.6
Japan	62.8	68.3	70.0	70.0
Non-EEC Europe	47.9	58.5	62.3	62.3

would regard an increase in spending as a cause of unemployment. The welfare state can play a special role because deductions are based on labor costs rather than on total revenue, and the extent of the deductions can therefore interfere with wage bargaining.

Unemployment Benefits
High unemployment benefits are often mentioned as another reason for the persistence of unemployment. Table 2.6 summarizes the available information on the "replacement rates" of individuals' incomes (unemployed individuals' incomes divided by their wages prior to layoff). The most striking feature of this table is the high degree of similarity of the data. With the exception of Japan, which has the most favorable conditions for the jobless, all countries seem to compensate their jobless in identical proportions: between 50 and 60 percent of their initial wages. (It should be noted that unemployment benefits have *increased* in non-EU European countries.) However, these data do not do justice to the significant differences in the length of time over which the jobless receive unemployment benefits.[9] In non-EU European countries benefits are given for less than a year, whereas the present system in the EU countries is much

more generous. But studies dealing with this issue are not very successful in tabulating the quantitative significance of this phenomenon.[10]

Disinflation

Can the reduction of the inflation rate during the 1980s be interpreted as the result of excessively austere public policies which would have precipitated the rise of European unemployment? Such an interpretation would be compatible with another one showing that the disequilibria of the 1970s (brought about by the oil crisis) might not necessarily be of the same nature as those of the 1980s and the 1990s (brought about, perhaps, by European deflationary policies).

The problem with this interpretation is that countries with low unemployment rates experience the same disinflation process as those with high unemployment rates. One would therefore have to imagine that EU countries would have had to work harder than others to achieve the same disinflation as other OECD countries. This would be a surprising outcome, insofar as EU countries are known to experience less nominal wage inertia vis-à-vis inflation than other OECD countries and, consequently, are in a better position for prompt adjustment to disinflation. It is therefore difficult to accept that the reduction of the inflation rate during the 1980s might account for a rise in unemployment during this same period.

The Labor "Market"

It is difficult to attribute rising unemployment in the European Union to an "external" cause. Whether one thinks of the oil crisis, the increase in taxation, or the elimination of jobs due to restructuring and technological progress, nothing distinguishes the EU countries from other OECD countries. One must therefore attempt to analyze unemployment in terms of endogenous causes linked to the different ways in which the labor market works in different countries.

What is the source of the differences in the way the labor market works? In their analysis of European unemployment, Bruno and Sachs use the notion of "corporatism" to refer to the modes of regulation of the labor market in countries (such as Scandinavian countries or Austria) in which wage bargaining is centralized.[11] In those countries, trade unions and governments make "collective" choices, taking into account the interests of the jobless as well as the interests of the employed. Unemployment is thus directly "internalized" by the decision makers. In their expansion of Bruno and Sachs's analyses, Calmfors and Drifill elaborate as follows[12]: Centralizing wage bargaining is a good thing insofar as it can lead to socially efficient tradeoffs between wages and jobs. At the other extreme, however, a totally competitive market can also allow prompt adjustments in employment. The pressure of competition forces a prompt adjustment of workers' wages and mobility to levels that make hiring the jobless profitable. The relationship between unemployment and centralized wage bargaining would thus resemble an inverted U curve. Both extremes (total centralization and complete decentralization) are good, but the intermediate situation that best characterizes the EU countries does not allow either of these kinds of arbitration. In the absence of sufficiently centralized bargaining, trade unions do not want to make efforts in their sectors if these efforts will benefit other sectors. In the absence of sufficiently strong competition, wage bargaining can respond only partially to disequilibria in the labor market. On the contrary, centralized bargaining makes workers accept wage (or fiscal) adjustments that are in the interest of those who are unemployed. At the other extreme, the stark reality of the market is such that wage adjustments promptly follow employment disequilibria.

The picture just sketched points to a first characteristic distinguishing the labor market within the European Union from the labor markets in other European countries, in Japan, and in the United States. Let us now analyze the specificity of European unemployment from another angle.

Insiders and Outsiders

Whatever its source may be, European unemployment's major feature is persistence. Particularly striking is the fact that there was no visible recovery of employment once the effects of the (oil, etc.) crises had been reversed in the second half of the 1980s. Several theories have attempted to account for such persistence. One of the most convincing is the theory of insiders and outsiders.[13]

According to this theory, there is not a single "labor market" in which supply and demand adjust to each other; there are several internal markets in which wages are determined so as to maintain the profitability of existing jobs. This argument is not in contradiction with a recent tendency to negotiate wage cuts in order to avoid unemployment (Volkswagen and Air France workers are recent examples); rather, it demonstrates it as a counterexample. Wage adjustments are possible when the jobs of employed workers are threatened. They are not when cuts are necessary to increase net job creation.

A central implication of this theory is that it is very difficult for unemployment to disappear as long as workers with jobs succeed in forming such a tight group that they are able to resist downward pressures which *outsiders* will try to impose on them to obtain a job. Whenever market conditions are good, wages adjust upward, as those who are employed stop fearing about the loss of their jobs. This prevents the unemployed from benefiting fully from the upturns of the cycles in order to get a job. Persistence, more than any other feature, therefore appears to be a specific characteristic of unemployment in the European Community. The jobless who have been excluded too long from the labor market practically do not participate any longer in seeking out the available job offers. Mechanisms of social and wage regulation operate without them.

One can now clearly sees the difference between the United States and Europe. In Europe a core of insiders have succeeded to resist the pressure of competition imposed on the labor markets by the cohorts of outsiders. This helped them to keep upward pressures on wages, despite the seemingly endless rise of unemployment. On the other hand, the United States kept putting pressure on the employed to leave room for the unemployed.

Unemployment or Inequalities

One could have expected that the U.S. model, being more competitive, would produce less income dispersion (for given skills everybody should earn the same) than in Europe (where wage earners should be highly dependent upon the productivity of the sector in which they work). It just comes out the opposite. Inequalities exploded in the United States in the 1980s; in Europe they have been rising only slightly. One explanation that comes to mind is that Europe imposes higher minimum wages than the United States, so that inequalities could not increase in Europe (where wages cannot go down much), while instead unemployment did rise. In Europe minimum wages and unemployment benefits certainly shut off access to underpaid jobs, which are typically available to the American labor force. These regulations, it should be emphasized, do not deter the secular mobility (from agriculture to industry, from industry to services, and so on) that was discussed above. Indeed, the "good jobs," as they are called in the United States (interestingly, in Europe "jobs" is the only word in use), are better paid than the jobs that they are substituted for, so minimum-wage laws should not be binding. But these regulations (minimum wage, unemployment benefits) do make it impossible to offer jobs that pay low wages, offer little opportunity for promotion, and require few skills—jobs that workers want to quit as soon as they can.

Although the "bad" jobs certainly contribute to the widening of wage inequalities in the United States, they do not explain everything. Indeed, the pattern of rising wage inequalities is observed in all segments of the wage distribution. Even "observationally identical" workers (meaning workers with the same education, sex, and age) have been subject to rising inequalities[14] (so the distinction between high wages and low wages does not, by itself, explain the pattern of U.S. inequalities). This points to two ideas. One is that the pressure of competition in the United States forces workers to take a job, whatever the wage, so that the lack (or the decline) of unions or the lack of minimum-wage regulation comes to be reflected in a wide disparity of earnings. The other idea is that the core of European insiders may not really be firm specific; it may be more economy wide than one might have believed. The European "insiders" do not necessarily keep their jobs. As the OECD Job Study (two volumes; Paris, 1994) reveals, worker turnover (including job-to-job mobility) is large in Europe. The key difference with the United States, as is apparent in table 2.2, is over the number of workers who leave a job and are unemployed before they get another job. In Europe, most mobility is job-to-job rather than job-to-unemployment-to-job.

Blanchard and Diamond develop a similar idea and present a model that distinguishes two types of outsiders: those who have just lost their jobs and those who have been unemployed for a long time.[15] If the jobless who have just entered the pool of the unemployed are the first to be rehired (because employers regard them as better qualified to fill positions), insiders will easily move from firm to firm. Wage bargaining will nevertheless remain at a high level, insofar as employed workers' fears of unemployment will never be such as to make them accept wages that would be compatible with hiring all the jobless.

The U.S. Productivity Slowdown Reconsidered

Although the European Union model appears clearly inefficient in terms of jobs, one must ponder another question: Is it inefficient in terms of growth? If one looks beyond the difference in unemployment between Europe and the United States and

Table 2.7
Growth rates of per-capita income (percent). Source: Angus Maddison, *Dynamic Forces Capitalist Development* (Oxford University Press, 1991).

	1950–1973	1973–1989
Germany	4.9	2.1
England	2.5	1.8
France	4.0	1.8
Japan	8.0	3.1
United States	2.2	1.6
OECD average	3.8	2.1

concentrates on output growth, one does not find much that would support the superiority of the U.S. model. As table 2.7 shows, growth in per-capita income (rather than growth per worker) is no less robust in Europe than in the United States.

In Europe, growth was achieved through large immaterial technical progress (which, by itself, explains as much as 50 percent of growth). In the United States, instead, growth was obtained through the growing number of jobs created (which, together with other material inputs, explains growth entirely[16]).

This comparison led some economists to go so far as to regard European unemployment as a model! Such is the point of view offered by Paul Romer, the inventor of the theory of endogenous growth, in his article "Crazy explanations for the productivity slowdown" (in *NBER Macroeconomics Annual 1987*). According to Romer, the better productivity of Europe and the worse productivity of the United States are endogenous features of the two labor markets. Europe, by choosing high wages, forces entrepreneurs to innovate so as to substitute new technologies for expensive workers; the United States, by taking the opposite route, discourages productivity growth. In the end, output does not turn out to be lower in Europe, despite the rising unemployment. This shows that unemployment is perhaps more a social problem than an economic one. A society in which the unemployed are so numerous, as in Europe, suffers less from the forgone growth than from the loss of social cohesion that the high unemployment brings.

A Social Munich?

Charles Bean concludes his study of European unemployment with a cryptic remark: "There is a large payoff to preventing unemployment [from] rising in the first place." We should hope that this truism has now become meaningful. Whichever social modalities it activates, whether it be straight laissez-faire or centralizing corporatism, a procedure is efficient if it eradicates unemployment at the base and "forcibly" (through market or institutional forces) reintegrates workers as soon as they lose their jobs. After a latency period, reentry becomes a much more painful process. The reason is that the jobless, especially those who have been unemployed for a long time, are gradually abandoned by the "insiders" and fall out of their sphere of regulation; the jobless themselves, for all practical purposes, disappear from the labor market.

Which side should one choose: laissez-faire, or corporatism? Neither way is easy. Consider first the course leaning toward corporatism, which the Scandinavian countries have followed. It is expensive to carry out "active" measures of support for the jobless (which include the hiring of many workers by the government) on the model of those developed in Sweden. In 1987 Sweden was spending 2 percent of its GDP on reentry programs for its jobless—almost the same rate at which Europe was spending on unemployment overall, although there was only one-fourth as much unemployment in Sweden.

The deep crisis in the Scandinavian countries in the early 1990s fully revealed the weaknesses of the corporatist approach. When faced with a financial crisis (triggered by unwise deregulation of financial markets), these countries experienced a tremendous upsurge in unemployment. The Swedish rate, which was equivalent to 3 percent of the working population in 1991, suddenly rose to approximately 10 percent in 1993; in Finland the unemployment rate jumped from 7 percent to 20 percent. The extent of the crisis now seems to exceed the capacities for fiscal absorption in these countries. After its public deficit reached 13 percent of the GDP, Sweden had to introduce austerity measures at the height of the crisis.

It is just as difficult to follow a course oriented to the liberal side of Calmfors and Driffill's curve. Mrs. Thatcher's England did not succeed in bringing unemployment anywhere near the U.S. level, despite all its efforts to obtain greater flexibility in the labor market. The reason is that laissez-faire weakens the whole society by forcing it to index costs and wages at a level compatible with full employment for all. The crisis of Reaganism, as crystallized in Clinton's election, demonstrated American society's impatience with a form of liberalism that sacrifices wages to employment.

In other words, whatever an ultra-liberal or an ultra-corporatist course may do to resolve the crisis, they both bring destabilizing elements into the war on unemployment. In one case those who have jobs are forced to compete with those who do not; in the other case, costly reentry programs for the jobless must be paid for.

The EU countries have remained in the middle. In these countries, unemployment has been feared less than the remedies that would have been necessary to contain it. The war on unemployment is in the hands of governments which represent first and foremost the point of view of the people who have jobs and fear losing them. Consequently, the other categories of social benefits (health care, pensions, aid to families) are given more importance. In France unemployment uses only a limited portion of the nation's social budget; it trails far behind pensions or health care and is almost on a par with aid to families. The sums of money allocated to employment policies are significant if compared to the budget for culture or justice; however, they are modest in comparison with the major sectors of government intervention. In contrast with pensioners or medical patients, or even construction lobbies, the jobless are only indirectly present when lobbying takes place.

This is probably what led Philippe Séguin, president of France's National Assembly, to call the attitude of governments in the face of unemployment a "social Munich."[17] (At Munich, in 1938, England and France essentially agreed to let Hitler take Czechoslovakia in order—they thought—to avoid war.) The blame may have been directed at Séguin's colleagues, but it should be directed at society as a whole—just as it probably should have been in 1938. For example in 1989–90, when French unemployment fell under 9 percent for a few months, there was an immediate pressure on wages and an increase in street demonstrations in favor of income growth. It was as if a 9 percent rate of unemployment was regarded as the "full employment" level of joblessness—on the basis of which a return to wage increases was possible again. Wages, which are frozen in periods of unemployment, are still indexed upward in periods of growth! This asymmetry sums up the tragedy of unemployment in the European Union.

Conclusion

The methods used by the societies that have escaped unemployment are radically different from one another. Some societies let competition put pressure on workers with jobs to force them to "make room" for unemployed workers. Others have collectively negotiated tradeoffs that have made for compatibility between jobs and wages.

The hybrid chosen by the European Union is the least efficient method. Unable to coordinate job creation at the social level or to accept imposing competition on the labor market, they have let themselves be trapped into a continuous rise in unemployment. Each step makes it harder to win the battle and makes a return to previous rates less likely. Long-term unemployment, which is properly speaking the trademark of European unemployment, results from these non-choices.

Should the European Union take the direction of laissez-faire? It tried to do so to an extent during the 1980s, but the fear of rising inequalities (at least for those who already have a job—the "insiders") kept the process from going very far. Should the EU go further in the direction of the Scandinavian model, and fight unemployment in a way that would somewhat parallel the "war on poverty" in the United States in the 1960s? Reentry programs for the long-term unemployed and subsidies directed toward the weaker segments of the labor market (the young and the long-term unemployed) have also been tried; however, such solidarity efforts are never going to go very far in an intermediate society where the market is tightly constrained by wage-bargaining procedures that operate mostly for the benefit of those who have jobs.

Is there another way out? Can't one imagine a welfare state of the twenty-first century that could efficiently solve these dilemmas? What about economic policy at large, and the Keynesian optimism over the role of the state? It is now time to review the role of the state in the working of a market economy.

Appendix to Chapter 2

Structure of the working population (in percent). Source: Angus Maddison, *Dynamic Forces in Capitalist Development* (Oxford University Press, 1991).

	Agriculture	Industry	Services
1950			
France	28.3	34.9	36.8
Germany	22.2	43.0	34.8
Japan	48.3	22.6	29.1
United Kingdom	5.1	46.5	48.4
United States	13.0	33.3	53.7
1973			
France	16.9	38.5	50.6
Germany	7.1	46.6	46.3
Japan	13.4	37.2	49.4
United Kingdom	2.9	41.7	55.4
United States	4.1	32.3	63.6
1990			
France	6.1	29.9	64.0
Germany	3.4	39.8	56.8
Japan	7.2	34.1	58.7
United Kingdom	2.1	29.0	68.9
United States	2.8	26.2	70.9

3

Keynes and His Shadow

Whatever role the state might have played in economic life in the past, there was always one major factor that limited the scope of its interventions. In pre-nineteenth-century rural societies, very few goods were traded, so the ability of the state to tax the economy could never go very far. In the nineteenth century, although the industrial revolution dramatically widened the scope of tradable activities (which could now be taxed), the role of the state stayed limited to a narrow range. For a time, the "laissez-faire" coalition resisted the demands of the urban working class and the gradually mounting threat of a socialist revolution to redistribute resources more actively.[1]

Against the skepticism of those who feared that democracies would lose the battle to totalitarian systems, John Maynard Keynes stands as the key thinker who convinced that proper government intervention could reconcile democracy and capitalism in a new world in which the democratic aspiration to well-being for all could be fulfilled through capitalism's full employment (rather than capitalism's disappearance).

The success of Keynes's ideas was immense, but there is some confusion between the success of his recipe and the success of the postwar recovery across the OECD countries. To some extent, it is now being discovered that the implementation of

Keynes's program was not so much the cause of postwar successes; rather, the brilliance of these years made it possible to put Keynes's ideas into practice.

The difference between Keynes's influence in the 1930s and his legacy in the 1950s is interesting. The Keynes who has become a part of history—the one who explained that all it takes to become affluent is to spend—is not the Keynes who told the policy makers of his time that new growth would require the expropriation of rentiers and other owners of the wealth that had been accumulated during the nineteenth century. Once the task of expropriation had been accomplished, it became possible for William Henry Beveridge to explain how to establish the welfare state on the post-World War II tabula rasa.

Economic Consequences of World War I

Keynes's intellectual history begins in 1919 with the publication of *The Economic Consequences of Peace*. Europe was bare, four empires had fallen, and the United States was becoming the center of the world. In this scene of dust and blood, Clémenceau, an old man whose most vivid impressions were those of his past, felt called upon to be a Pericles whose "theory of politics was Bismarck's." This man "had one illusion—France; and one disillusion—mankind (including Frenchmen, and his colleagues not least)." Clémenceau was obsessed with destroying Germany, which he compared to a vast coal and steel manufacture; as a result, he made sure that the Treaty of Versailles would stipulate the following:

Germany must surrender most of its merchant fleet; it must hand over to the Allies the administration of the Oder, Rhine, and Danube rivers; it must cede its rights and titles to its overseas possessions while the

Allies maintain the right to expropriate—as reparation payments for war damages—any new titles acquired abroad by German residents.

Germany must cede to France all rights to exports from the Saar Basin mines; Upper Silesia must be handed back to Poland after a plebiscite; Germany must compensate France for its loss of coal through the destruction of its mines, as calculated in terms of their prewar profitability; it must furnish the Allies with 25,000,000 tons of coal annually for 10 years; and it must accord most-favored-nation treatment to the Allies, as it had before the war (with Alsace and Lorraine remaining free to export without payment of customs duty).

After fulfilling all these conditions, Germany will have to pay the equivalent of £1,000,000,000 before May 1, 1921, the Allies being empowered to demand payment in any manner they may see fit. This first billion pounds will be followed by four more, which may finally be supplemented by any sum deemed necessary to compensate civilian populations for damages resulting from the war. (For the sake of comparison, Keynes estimated that the compensations paid by Bismarck to France would have been equivalent to £500,000,000 in 1919.)

This extravagant list gives an idea of the excessiveness that prevailed during the First World War and the interwar years and sheds light on the unrealistic nature of the decisions made in Versailles. Clémenceau wanted to be absolutely sure to bridge forever the gap Germany had created between itself and France (in 1870 the two nations had comparable wealth; in 1914 Germany was leading by more than 70 percent). I need not elaborate on Keynes's prescience. By playing the sorcerer's apprentice and trying to deprive Germany of any hope of resurrection, the Allies pushed Germany in another direction, as forecast by Keynes.

The Euthanasia of Rentiers

Wars are usually financed through loans which are gradually paid off in postwar times. This is the reason why postwar economic conditions quickly turn gloomy. In the nineteenth century, government expenditures consisted mostly of public debt reimbursements or war expenditures. Public spending therefore consisted mainly in paying for past wars or preparing for future wars. Clémenceau and the politicians of his time continued thinking in those terms. The Treaty of Versailles was meant to make the vanquished pay for the war and to delay the advent of the next conflict. The twentieth century was viewed in terms of the model inherited from the nineteenth century. Against this background, Keynes would try to convince policy makers that Germany did not have the financial capacity to pay its war debts and that the winners would therefore have to pay for the war themselves—which they could do only by taxing the productive classes of the nation (wage earners) or by taxing the parasites (rentiers). In the former case the future is sacrificed on the altar of the past; in the latter case one turns the page on a bygone century and builds strong foundations for the new century. Consequently, Keynes made these simple political economic recommendations to the governments of his time: War debts should be thrown into "a general bonfire," the gold parity of currencies should be sharply reduced so that the public debts would be proportionately reduced, and that would be the end of war debts. At the time when he was writing against the Treaty of Versailles, Keynes—just like the main character in *The Leopard*—may have been thinking that everything must change so that everything can remain the same.

But governments did not see it that way. Without exception, the great men whose names today fill the pages of history books because a war was won thanks to their resolve in the face of adversity wanted at first to preserve the past and made efforts to restore the gold convertibility of their currencies. Such a policy only serves to defend the purchasing power of rentiers, the people who can really gain from it. But, as Keynes would say, the Italians were fortunate that the value of a currency is not established by decree and "the lira does not listen even to a dictator." The French were also fortunate that "one blames politicians, not for inconsistency, but for obstinacy"[2]—this allowed Poincaré to declare that "it would be an act of national bankruptcy and shame to devalue the Franc" and to make threats of resignation (after devaluation) "against anyone who would hinder him in so good a deed."

It was unfortunate for England that the myth of the Almighty Sterling and the illusion of defending those who save money against the vicissitudes of history led Chancellor of the Exchequer Winston Churchill to commit the economic crime of restoring the pound to its prewar parity. Keynes's interpretation of such a policy was that, by forcing prices and wages down, it transferred wealth to rentiers, who could benefit from it because their income *increased* as a result of lower prices. According to Keynes, rentiers thus gained approximately £1,000,000,000, to the detriment of the productive classes of the nation. "The economic consequences of Mr. Churchill"[3] were severe: 25 percent unemployment in 1930 and possibly some indirect responsibility in the course of events that led to the 1929 crash. England, by protecting its rentiers from war-induced bankruptcy, sacrificed its productive classes.

Keynes's most famous pronouncements originated in this polemic against rentiers, which paved the way for his work as an economist. Rentiers constituted, in his words, "a large, powerful, and greatly respected class of persons, well-to-do individually and very wealthy in the aggregate, who owned neither buildings, nor land, nor businesses, nor precious metals, but titles to an annual income in legal-tender money,"[4] which increases over time without any effort on the part of its owner. Rentiers show the other face of capitalism. Capitalists start out as entrepreneurs when they invest their money, then promptly turn into rentiers once they claim the fruit of their savings for themselves or their children. Keynes's scorn for rentiers brings him close to Marx's view of capital as "dead," frozen labor that no longer produces the "surplus value" on which the owner still claims payment. It also brings Keynes close, possibly closest, to Malthus, who was pondering the stability of a society that would be concerned only with saving and never with consuming.[5]

The General Theory

Defending rentiers is in fact defending a principle whose time has passed, namely saving. "The morals, the politics, the literature, and the religion of the age joined in a grand conspiracy for the promotion of saving. . . . A rich man could, after all, enter into the Kingdom of Heaven—if only he saved." These words, written by Keynes in the 1920s, paved the way for his magnum opus, *The General Theory of Employment, Interest and Money* (1936), in which he echoed Malthus by saying that "the principles of saving, pushed to excess, would destroy the motive to production. If every person were satisfied with the simplest food, the poorest clothing, and the meanest houses, it is certain that no other sort of food, clothing and lodging would be in existence."

When individuals save money, they may be thinking of consuming later, and a rational use for their savings is probably to invest today in order to satisfy this deferred increase in consumption tomorrow. If Robinson Crusoe decides to fish less today (and reduce his current consumption of fish) in order to take the time to make a fishing rod or nets so as to increase his productive capacity tomorrow, saving and investing are a single act for him: he reduces his consumption and simultaneously increases his investment. This is not the way it works in a decentralized capitalist society. A fisherman who observes that the demand for fish is declining today is entitled to wonder if the demand will increase tomorrow, in which case he should use his available resources to increase his capacity to supply and "take advantage" of this lower demand to make fishing rods. Suppose that he does not think so and allows others to take care of investing. Suppose, further, that all producers are similarly affected by a "confidence crisis" (as was certainly the case in the 1930s). Consumers become cautious and save. Firms also become cautious and prefer to postpone investing. This creates a disequilibrium: savers want to buy securities, which firms do not need since they do not wish to invest.

In theory, such a disequilibrium should make the prices of securities go up, bring down interest rates and encourage firms to invest.[6] In opposition to this idyllic sequence, Keynes offers the following: If firms do not want to invest and consumers do not want to consume, firms will find themselves in a position of having excessive productive capacity. They will lay off in the adversely affected sector (in this case the sector of ordinary consumer goods) *without* hiring in the sector that should benefit from it, namely the sector of investment goods. Layoffs will make income go down. Through this lowering of income they trigger a second wave of reduction in spending: households are now poorer as a result of layoffs and will consume even less. This "crisis" atmosphere will not encourage firms to invest either. At the end of a process in which the initial disequilibrium may be *multiplied* to a considerable extent, a new equilibrium will emerge; but it will be an *underemployment equilibrium* in which both the production level and the income level will have been adjusted downward.

Thus, unemployment presents itself as a result of undercon-sumption—in the words of Sismondi, an effect of the tyranny of saving over a society that has too much of it. Getting rid of unemployment therefore requires a simple remedy: money has to be spent, at any cost, even if it means hiring unemployed individuals to fill in the afternoon the holes they dug that same morning. Even better, in order to avoid the crisis multiplier, the income of individuals should be dissociated from their employ-ment as much as possible. By thus separating employment and income, one avoids having unemployment force the jobless to reduce their spending; the crisis multiplier is reduced and the economy is stabilized. The Keynesian message of the welfare state was to be delivered by another Englishman: Beveridge, who, for all practical purposes, becomes one with Keynes, like a shadow, in discussions of Keynesianism.

The Welfare State and Its Genesis

Churchill had learned the Keynesian lesson through the crisis. In November 1940, as the war was raging, he ordered a report on ways to cope with the social consequences of the crisis of the 1930s as well as those resulting from the war. The report was made public in 1942. In the report, Beveridge spelled out the principles—essentially ours today—to be followed by a government in its obligation to society to fight the five scourges of mankind, namely "want, disease, ignorance, squalor and idleness."[7]

In Beveridge's formulation the welfare state is not a conduit for the generosity of the wealthiest toward the poorest; rather, it is a way of protecting society as a whole against itself. After being convinced by Keynes that the only possible reason for society to become poor is insufficient spending, Beveridge felt entitled to request that minimal spending be guaranteed by the government. Hence the title he gave his report: Full Employment in a Free Society. This emblematic title was to become the hallmark of postwar "Keynesianism." Beveridge's welfare state was turning its back on the past, building on what was now (financially) a blank postwar slate (since the winners had understood the lessons of World War I); it would gradually come to occupy the vacuum created by the rentiers of the early part of the century. The great French historian Lucien Febvre, when asked in the 1950s about the most significant event in the century, named the disappearance of rentiers. Early in the century their revenues corresponded to approximately 30 percent of the income of most European nations; today it only amounts to a few percentage points of it. Inversely, government welfare expenditures represented a few percentage points in the early part of the century; today they represent close to 30 percent in most European countries. Yesterday's rentiers have been replaced by the beneficiaries of the welfare state. There is a name for the difference between the two: democracy, which gives to most what had been reserved for a few.

The historical changes introduced by Beveridge (by "Keynesianism") were less radical than is usually thought. It is the whole twentieth century, rather than just the postwar years, that bears testimony to the "great transformation" of society in the direction of the welfare state.

The Century of the Welfare State

The welfare state is not exactly an invention of Keynesianism. The idea already existed before the 1930s. Without going into the details of its genesis, we can at least give credit to Bismarck for one of the founding projects. Indeed, as early as 1883, Bismarck pushed to a vote one of the very first social laws in favor of workers; it established compulsory medical insurance for Germany's low-wage laborers—a move that was to be followed and expanded in all other industrialized countries. In Bismarck's famous words, "The democrats will play flute when the people understands that it is the Prince who takes cares of its interest." On the eve of World War I, Great Britain, France, and the United States had all voted in social laws.

In a retrospective table of public expenditures, Christine André and Robert Delorme propose a typology that breaks government expenditures down into four general categories: political, economic, social, and debt.[8] Political expenditures include military and police expenditures. . . . Economic expenditures essentially consist of aid to industry. Social expenditures include both social welfare expenditures (health care, aid to families, pensions, unemployment benefits) and educational expenditures. Let us examine here the data concerning the United Kingdom because it is Keynes's and Beveridge's country and also because these data show the most regular progression.

Table 3.1 reveals remarkable continuity. Public expenditures represented 10 percent of GDP at the beginning of the century, 20 percent of it immediately after World War I, 30 percent immediately after World War II, and 40 percent in 1970. At the dawn of the 1980s it represented 45 percent of GDP, at which point it leveled off (as in all other countries). As one sees, the figures do not really show any abrupt change that could be associated with either Keynes or Beveridge.

Let us now examine the composition of expenditures. Table 3.2 highlights the fact that the proportion of social expenditures doubled once between 1900 and 1938, then almost doubled again between 1938 and 1980. Once more, it is tempting to see continuity rather than discontinuity.

Table 3.1
Public expenditures in United Kingdom as percentage of GDP. Source: Christine André and Robert Delorme. "Matériaux pour une comparaison internationale des dépenses publiques en longue période. Le cas de six pays industrialisés," in *Statistiques et Etudes Financières* (Ministère de l'Economie et des Finances, 1983).

1900	1920	1938	1950	1960	1970	1980
10.3	20.1	28.9	28.9	32.6	39.3	44.6

Table 3.2
Composition of public expenditures in United Kingdom as percentage of total expenditures. Source: Christine André and Robert Delorme. "Matériaux pour une comparaison internationale des dépenses publiques en longue période. Le cas de six pays industrialisés," in *Statistiques et Etudes Financières* (Ministère de l'Economie et des Finances, 1983).

	1900	1920	1938	1950	1970	1980
Political	57.8	39.4	36.3	28.0	22.2	20.5
Economic	17.2	14.4	12.8	14.7	13.0	9.0
Social	18.0	25.9	37.6	46.1	55.0	60.1
Debt	7.0	20.4	13.4	11.2	9.9	10.3

What does this progression tell us? First of all, it emphasizes how much things have changed. At the beginning of the century public expenditures represented 10 percent of GDP; at the end of the century it represents 45 percent of it. From John Lackland's difficulties in convincing English barons to accept the scutage to the lengthy acceptance of the income tax, the history of taxation[9] shows how difficult it has been for the nation-states to avail themselves of the technical and political instruments of modern taxation.

The twentieth century allowed governments to play a much more important role. Both World War I and World War II contributed to this in a fundamental way by raising the proportion of public expenditures and taxation to levels from which they were not to come down. In the aftermath of the wars, social expenditures slowly but surely came to replace military expenditures. But, as table 3.2 shows, social expenditures (including educational expenditures) were gradually rising even before World War II. This process continued immediately after World War II. In Great Britain the proportion of public expenditures was still at the same level in 1960 as it had been in 1938, but the proportion of social expenditures (as a percentage of the GDP) had already doubled.

Then came the 1960s, when there was (in all countries) a new round of increases in the proportion of public expenditures as a percentage of GDP (in spite of the latter's rapid increase). It was the golden age of "Keynesianism." Keynes's principles explicitly inspired John F. Kennedy's program; as soon as he was elected, he decided to lower taxes in order to boost the economy. Lyndon B. Johnson, following in Beveridge's footsteps, created Medicare and Medicaid to give social coverage to old and poor people. The increase in public expenditures was openly guided by a search for "new [domestic] frontiers" (to put it in President Johnson's terms).

However, the increase in the amount of public expenditures was not always guided by a "program." Governments often had to accept it. As Delorme and André demonstrated, the welfare state almost imposed itself: over time, society has claimed more and more rights to education, health care, and pensions, and these claims have always exceeded governmental "programs."[10] There is no doubt that "Keynesianism" helped, at the intellectual level, to make it easier for this development to be accepted. At the same time, it is clear that the increase in social expenditures first corresponded to "needs" (for medical insurance, old-age insurance, and so on) much more than it did to a program of Keynesian regulation of the economy—even though such a policy was at times also present (as in the case of President Kennedy's tax cuts).

Let us first examine, without going into all the details of its various categories, the most illustrative of these processes: health insurance.

Health Insurance

In his attempt to close the Reagan years, Bill Clinton made of health coverage the one item where government action was needed. It is indeed the sector in which the comparison of the United States with Europe is the most striking. In contrast with European countries overall, the United States has only lately and partially been tempted by the welfare state. The idea started blossoming there in the mid 1960s (once more in the midst of a war, in this case the Vietnam War). The "Great Society" program launched by President Johnson did not take the overall shape that was characteristic of the European welfare state. As far as health was concerned, the program was limited to granting aid to the poorest (the Medicaid program) and the oldest (the Medicare program). As a result, public expenditures were significantly lower in the United States than in European countries: 31 percent and 43 percent respectively in the late 1980s. Most of the difference has to do with health care, which is essentially public in Europe and essentially private in the United States.

The American system of health insurance costs much more than its European counterpart. The U.S. figure of 12.5 percent of GDP for 1990 is almost 50 percent higher than the European figure. This is first a lesson to the Europeans: the rising share of the welfare state cannot be attributed solely to the government. Rather, it reflects much more clearly the fulfillment of a need (receiving medical care and being assured of a guaranteed income in old age) that private American insurance companies were happy to satisfy when the government had not committed to doing so.

It is easy to trace the origin of these new needs. The spectacular transformations that have occurred in medicine since World War II have resulted in a spectacular increase in life expectancy; at the same time, they have led to a much higher number of medical transactions and a considerable increase in the capital intensity of medicine.

But the difference between the U.S. and European numbers is also a lesson for the United States. It shows that governments can be more efficient in regulating spending that the private sector. In order to understand why, one can read Kenneth Arrow's "Uncertainty and the welfare economics of medical care" (*American Economic Review* 53 (1963): 941–973), a paper that paved the way for the field of health economics.

Arrow summarizes the particular problem raised by medical costs as follows: Health care is one of the few economic goods for which (the patient's) demand depends entirely on the evaluation of it by the (physician) supplier. Here demand is dictated by supply for the obviously perverse reason that the demander does not know what he wants. Anyone who has ever questioned an auto mechanic's honesty knows what Arrow means. However, one cannot acquire a new body the way one can acquire a new car. As a result, people usually do not dare question their doctor's diagnosis. The perverse mechanism identified by Arrow is obviously reinforced insofar as health-care costs are automatically covered by public or private insurance (few would want to take the risk of dying of appendicitis for lack of financial resources). Not only do people dare not question a physician's diagnosis; they have no incentive to do so, given the insurance coverage. Thus, health-care costs are driven up by a dual mechanism: the supplier dictates consumption to the demander, and a third party (the insurer) pays for the transaction.

A few studies will suffice to demonstrate the validity of Arrow's analysis.[11] An American study analyzed the appendectomy rate and the rate of mortality resulting from appendicitis in 23 New York hospitals. The appendectomy rate ranged from 2.9 percent in the poorest neighborhoods to 7.1 percent in the wealthiest neighborhoods. However, no relationship was found between the appendectomy rate and mortality due to appendicitis. Another study (quoted in Aaron's survey) analyzed 13 medical centers in a region of Vermont in which the population is very homogeneous in terms of income, social environment, and aggregate rate of disease. In spite of the overall homogeneity of the population, the number of surgical operations was twice as high in some medical facilities and the rate was directly related to the number of surgeons associated with each facility.

Many other examples also lead to the same conclusion: that the bias pointed out by Arrow is an important determining factor in medical costs. Its significance has been quantified in some American econometric studies: they reveal an elasticity of 0.55 between health-care costs and the number of practicing physicians in a given region. In other words, a 10 percent increase in the number of physicians working in a region contributes to a 5.5 percent increase in health-care costs in that particular region.

Health care is an exemplary component of the European welfare state. As compared to the American health-care system, the European system is both more egalitarian (almost everyone is covered in most European countries, whereas 40 million Americans have no social coverage at all) and cheaper (health-care costs represent approximately 12.5 percent of the United States' GDP, versus only about 8 percent of the GDP in European countries). This last feature is consistent with Arrow's finding that, in the absence of overall regulation, health-care costs are left to the discretion of health professionals. Beyond this point, however, one can see that the comparison of Europe with the United States shows that the European welfare state has only satisfied a social demand, rather than truly controlling or guiding it. An increase in the demand for health care is to be expected in a society that is becoming wealthy, and the government can only act as a moderator, not as an instigator, of its excesses.

Old-Age Insurance

To analyze old-age insurance I shall use a model, developed by Paul Samuelson[12] and Maurice Allais,[13] that could be called "the generational dilemma." Loleh Bellon's play *De si Tendres Liens* [*Such Tender Ties*] illustrates its logic perfectly. The characters in this play are two women, a mother and her daughter, in two different periods of their lives. In the first period the mother is a young divorcee and her daughter is a child. All the dialogues associated with this period have more or less the same content: the daughter wants her mother to stay home and take care of her instead of going out with men in the evening. The second period occurs 25 years later. (The play is constructed in such a way that one can never immediately place a dialogue in time.) The daughter's preoccupations are her husband, her children, and her job; the mother has grown old. The dialogues associated with this period also have a uniform content: the mother is asking her daughter to stay with her and not abandon her to her solitude.

The charm of this play lies in that it continually alternates between these two periods. The same dialogues occur 25 years apart, only the roles are reversed. Each of the two women is asking for the same thing at two different times: to be loved by the other one. If they were the same age, things would be simple: their reciprocal love would be reinforced, here and now. The problem with intergenerational love is that there is never a "coincidence of needs" (to put it in economic terms).

This frustration appears particularly disturbing in Bellon's play because it also shows how simple it would be for the mother to give more time to her daughter and for the daughter to do so for her mother. Indeed it seems that it would not take much for this reciprocal love to free itself from the restraint imposed by the age difference. All that is really needed is for these women to have access to what takes place in most families in which people love one another without any distinction between generations—in which parents love their children as well as their own parents, forming a generational chain that assures them of being later loved by their grown children.

These women have no access to the generational chain because they are caught in a dual relationship. The mother does not love her daughter enough (and tries to get remarried) because she knows (fears) that, later on, her daughter will pull away from her in order to pursue her own life. Knowing this, the mother—as a young woman—makes it a priority to take care of herself and thus makes her prediction come true. A third entity is needed (an institution assured of permanence, the "family") in order for each generation to receive from the following one what it gave to the preceding one—an institution in which children "reward" with their love the love that their parents gave to their own parents. In the absence of such an intergenerational chain, each loves the other one (of course), but the frustration shown by Loleh Bellon prevents this love from freeing itself of "here and now" constraints.

Economic Interpretation

Each of the two characters in the play is limited to a "here and now" (affective) exchange, and the time constraint prevents love from developing along richer intergenerational lines. Are exchanges between generations of a different nature in the purely economic domain? Each generation (directly or indirectly) produces economic goods with which to buy other goods. An auto worker uses his money to buy bread, which is sold to him by a baker who will use his earnings to buy a car. Putting aside the manufacturing time needed to produce the goods, these exchanges are examples of a simultaneous nature of needs, their co-occurrence in time—which is why Adam Smith had no doubt that each individual would be satisfied with his or her exchanges with others.

Let us now assume that an agent's actions, rather than consisting entirely of working (today) in order to immediately consume goods produced by others, are also oriented to the future. If an agent works today in order to consume *tomorrow,* he has to save, and that means acquiring claims on the rest of society that will give him a livelihood once he retires. Let us assume for now that a social security system does not exist; let us further assume that all goods are perishable, making it impossible to buy today economic goods that can be used tomorrow. How can one save under such conditions? There is only one way: finding another agent and lending him one's savings in exchange for reimbursement in the future. It turns out that this apparently simple act is always economically impossible for one generation as a whole, for the same reasons that were present in Loleh Bellon's play.

Let us assume, for the sake of demonstration, that society consists of only two types of agents: young people and old people. Young people want to save in order to finance their retirement. Other agents to whom they can lend must be found, directly or indirectly. Who will they be? Not other young people, who are also concerned about consuming less than they earn. Not old people, either—how could they reimburse their debt? When the young people have become old and want to cash in their claims, the old people will have died and will not be there to pay them back. As soon as economic relations between generations try to break away from the simultaneous nature of the purchase and sale of a commodity, they run the risk of facing an intergenerational gap exactly identical to the one illustrated by Loleh Bellon's play.

Let us now assume that this society (which consists of a constantly renewed pair of one young and one old generation) decides to have a government. Let us further assume that this government forces young people to give 20 percent of their earnings to old people. The net result of what looks like expropriation of their earnings by a heavy-handed government is to give young people access to intergenerational exchanges from which they were barred by the sheer logic of the market. Indeed, once they get old they will in turn receive 20 percent of the earnings of (new) young people. The contribution required by the government (provided that it was set at an appropriate level) enables them to achieve an otherwise impossible intergenerational exchange. Each generation gives to the preceding one and receives from the following one. The balance of purchases and sales from one pair of generations to another is never closed. Each generation is a creditor to the preceding one and a debtor to the following one. As in the case of the intergenerational love produced by a family (of which the two women in the play are deprived), individuals receive from one generation and give to another.

The welfare state, which is based on solidarity between working and retired individuals (as well as between the sick and the healthy and between the unemployed and the employed) can therefore be characterized as the accomplishment at the societal level of an intergenerational solidarity which could not be accomplished by any market logic. One can see that it is not governed at all by a logic of "hidden" expropriation. On the contrary, the welfare state functions better insofar as it is made perfectly transparent. Young people are happy to contribute as long as they know that they will later be compensated with the contributions of the future younger generation. Far from being a zero-sum game (in which one takes from Peter to give to Paul), the welfare state is a positive-sum game. All individuals benefit from a gift from the following generation which offsets—in terms of welfare—the gift they made to the preceding generation.

The Crisis of "Pay-As-You-Go" Systems

"Pay-as-you-go" systems (which correspond to the scheme we have analyzed so far: retired individuals receive contributions from the working population) compete with pension funds (in which retired individuals receive their *own* contributions plus the accrued interest which their retirement system will have earned in financial markets). Let us see what makes either of these two scheme more attractive.

When using Loleh Bellon's play as a starting point to demonstrate that the welfare state enables all generations to receive more than they give, we assumed that commodities cannot be directly saved for later consumption. We assumed that, in order to save, economic agents had to find another agent to whom they could lend—in other words, another agent who is willing to consume more today and less tomorrow. In practice, this is obviously a wrong hypothesis, since there are some durable goods, namely investments. Investments enable a society to accumulate today resources that—together with others—allow the production of other goods later.

Thus, in practice the choice that contributors have is not the one described above. The working population can either make contributions to the welfare state or buy capital (that is, securities which directly or indirectly provide them with a claim on future production). The possibility for the welfare state to be a positive-sum game is then dependent on a comparison of the "returns" one can expect from each of these two choices. If financial securities have a "low" yield, the welfare state will—as intuition tells us—maintain its superiority: accumulating financial assets in preparation for one's retirement will be less profitable than contributing to a social security system based on the distribution model. If, on the other hand, financial assets have a "high" yield (in relation to the product of interests available in financial markets), pension funds will be superior. More specifically, pay-as-you-go systems will dominate pension funds if the growth rate of the economy is higher than the yield offered in financial markets. Indeed, in this case future contributions grow more rapidly than the returns one receives by investing one's own contributions in financial markets.

The latter case prevailed from the early 1950s to the mid 1970s. The growth rates of most OECD countries were between 3 and 5 percent, while real interest rates (adjusted for inflation) were between 1 and 3 percent. In the 1980s the hierarchy was reversed as a result of the persistent slowdown in economic growth and the rising yields of financial securities. The efficiency of intergenerational redistributions, which supported the ascendancy of the welfare state during periods of strong growth, is now diminishing. In the 1980s, working individuals chose to keep their savings to themselves and invest them in financial markets, rather than "give them" to the unproductive population (in exchange for a later transfer of the same nature). If I expect the working population's income to be "low" in the year 2000, I will want to leave the chain of intergenerational solidarity which the welfare state wants to impose on me.

The Crisis in Public Finance

In the 1960s, when governments were concerned about containing the rising costs of the welfare state and controlling the public deficit, they were in fact more often concerned about possible effects on inflation or the balance of payments than about the threat that the rising public debt might pose to their own solvency. Indeed, economic growth seemed to guarantee that there would never be a problem of insolvency for the government. For example, public debt represented 100 percent of England's GNP in 1950. By 1975 it had gone down to 30 percent even though the government had never run a surplus; the denominator had simply always grown faster than the numerator.

The slow growth and the high interest rates that industrial countries experienced in the 1980s have invalidated this logic. The countries in which the public debt now exceeds the GDP are concerned about not being able to control it. It is suddenly becoming obvious that the welfare state was made possible by fast economic growth, rather than (as Keynesians believed) by economic growth resulting from the welfare state.

In a period of rapid growth, government bonds are secured by strong wealth *to come;* as a result, the government is freed of the risk of seeing a generation refuse to honor the claims accumulated by the preceding generation. On the other hand, in a period of slow growth, government bonds are burdened again by something Keynesianism thought it had eliminated: the increase in the government debt (in relation to the GDP) stands in the way of unceasing attempts to contain government deficits. In a period of slower growth, government deficits play only a transitory (though not necessarily negligible) role, and they no longer function as a recourse against a persistent slow-down in growth.

Conclusion

This new area of constraint, the rediscovery of public budgetary constraints burdening governments, is what I call the "crisis of Keynesianism." For the first time since the appearance of Keynes's ideas, in spite of the increasing power of a fiscal system freed of the straitjacket that had confined it until the nineteenth century, most governments have been constrained to contain their spending. Today they have to *arbitrate* between different areas (health care or education, the military or retire-ment programs, etc.), failing which they can follow the Ameri-can example and arbitrate over time by spending during one decade and reimbursing during the next.

But the Reagan years have left no place for Reagan's succes-sors to go. For at least a decade (the reverse of the flamboyant

Reagan decade), Americans have to pay off their debts. The burden of interest has already become the highest portion of public expenditures. One temptation is clearly to wipe out these debts by raising inflation. The monetary orthodoxy that gained new vigor in the 1980s all over the world stands in the way of such remedies. Is the crisis of economic policy ineluctably caught in the snare of slow growth and high interest rates, or can a new ("post-") Keynesianism be expected to renew the demand for state intervention?

Appendix

The following table gives the compositions of public expenditures (in percent) in France, Germany, and the United States. (Source: Christine André and Robert Delorme, "Matériaux pour une comparaison internationale des dépenses publiques en longue période. Le cas de six pays industrialisés," in *Statistiques et Etudes Financières* (Ministère de l'Economie et des Finances, 1983).)

France

	1872	1912	1920	1930	1938
Political	46.5	55.3	56.8	55.1	56.7
Economic	7.3	11.1	12.3	7.6	8.2
Social	4.7	14.2	7.8	13.9	15.9
Debt	41.5	19.4	23.1	23.4	18.2
Total (% of GDP)	11.0	12.8	32.8	21.9	26.5
	1950	1960	1970	1980	
Political	37.0	49.7	38.8	38.0	
Economic	30.3	14.8	20.1	15.2	
Social	28.6	31.2	37.2	45.2	
Debt	4.1	4.3	3.9	4.2	
Total (% of GDP)	41.1	38.6[a] (46.4[b])	40.1	48.3	

Germany

	1881	1910	1925	1930	1938
Political	70.6	49.6	24.3	19.9	
Economic	16.6	21.8	8.1	7.7	
Social	7.7	22.6	67.1	70.5	
Debt	5.2	6.0	0.4	1.9	
Total (% of GDP)	6.7	12.1[c]	30.3	43.1	48.2
	1950	1960	1970	1980	
Political	23.2	31.5	18.9	17.5	
Economic	9.6	15.6	13.4	10.1	
Social	65.6	50.0	65.5	68.9	
Debt	1.6	2.0	2.3	3.5	
Total (% of GDP)	41.8	32.0[d] (43.8[e])	37.6	46.9	

United States

	1872	1912	1920	1930	1938
Political		46.2	36.0	36.3	30.3
Economic		20.1	20.0	19.3	27.8
Social		27.4	27.5	32.2	32.0
Debt		6.2	16.6	12.1	9.9
Total (% of GFP)	4.5[f]	8.0	11.1	18.5	17.8
	1950	1960	1970	1980	
Political	70.6[g]	54.8[g]	34.0	25.8	
Economic	9.9	13.2	12.0	9.2	
Social	19.4	32.0	47.2	57.4	
Debt			6.8		
Total (% of GDP)	26.8	27.8	32.2	33.2	

a. New data on French GDP.
b. Old data on French GDP.
c. 1907.
d. Change in base.
e. New base.
f. Federal expenditures only.
g. Debt included.

4

The New Monetarist Orthodoxy

Keynes's conclusion to the *General Theory* contains a now famous statement: "Practical men, who believe themselves to be quite exempt from any intellectual influences, are usually the slaves of some defunct economist." As it turned out, throughout the 1960s and the 1970s policy makers became the "slaves" of none other than Keynes (something he must have thought of when he wrote that line). Slow growth and tight budget constraints put an end to Keynesian optimism. The crisis of the 1970s burned out government's margins of action and brought economic policy into the crisis that it was supposedly in charge of fighting. This led to a new orthodoxy, which was developed earlier but which took effect fully during the 1980s; for lack of a better term, it will be called the "new monetarism." Policy makers became slaves to this monetary orthodoxy, which called for government to stand back and abandon Keynes's call for intervention.

Words were not always followed by actions, but Ronald Reagan's and Margaret Thatcher's "laissez-faire" dogma set the example. In the 1980s the inflation of the 1970s was eradicated (one key goal of the monetarist program). This was also a time when important institutional reforms aimed at limiting the role of government were put in place. Privatization programs began multiplying all over the world (even in Argentina, where the Peronists had always opposed it before). In Europe, the Maastricht Treaty ratified the monetarist orthodoxy of the Bundesbank, making it a central tenet of the new Europe that price stability should be the only objective of the European Central Bank.

The rise of this new monetarist orthodoxy clearly bears the stamp of the inflationary 1970s. But it goes beyond the fight against inflation, castigating the very notion of government intervention. It even goes so far as to argue that government's hands have to be tied in advance in order to ensure that the state, like Ulysses, will resist the temptation to lose control of itself.

Is this new monetarism just a short-lived trend that will die once price stability is achieved and once public opinion and governments want to take bolder measures to fight unemployment? Or should the monetarist critique of Keynesian policy, which would sanction the failure of the welfare state, be considered a new element that is here to stay? In order to answer these questions, I will first try to show how monetarism, beyond the particular motive that gave rise to it (fighting the inflation of the early 1970s), has profoundly renewed the way to think of the government's position and role in economics. The arguments in favor of the idea that government's hands should be tied, which would be totally incomprehensible to a Keynesian of the old school, bring some profound insights to the understanding of the pros and cons of government regulation. I shall develop these ideas in an attempt to understand Europe's attempts to build up a supra-national government. On the other hand, I shall also try to show that government *non-intervention* can go much too far and end up being counterproductive if its scope is unlimited. This will be illustrated by

the example of the developing countries' debt crisis of the
1980s.

The Monetarist Critique of Keynesianism

Around the mid 1960s, the attempt to have "full employment"
ran into the problem of inflation. As the economies got near
full employment, tensions over wages intensified and brought
prices up; as a result, the objective of employment stabilization
came into conflict with the objective of price stabilization. This
tradeoff between inflation and unemployment has been characterized as a "Phillips curve"—named after the economist who
was the first to draw a curve representing this negative correlation over a span of more than a century. For Keynesians who
take this correlation into account, the master's philosophy is
essentially unchanged. One can always get closer to full employment by using the instruments of fiscal or monetary policy,
but it is up to governments to decide where to stop. When
inflationary pressures build up, they must learn to be cautious
and ease off their attempt to grow too fast.

This debate over the Phillips curve paved the way for the new
monetarism, which, after being introduced by Milton Friedman
in the 1960s and further developed by the Chicago economists
in the 1970s, came to be the major paradigm in economic
thought in the 1980s. Although the monetarist school is far
from being homogeneous (the term itself was introduced by
Karl Brunner in 1968 and never really accepted by his colleagues), I shall merely use it as a brand name for various
authors who expressed skepticism toward inflation and government regulation.

Let me begin with Friedman's analysis of the Phillips curve.[1]
First, call the "natural" rate of unemployment the rate of

unemployment for which no tension on the labor market
emerges: firms and workers are content with the prices and
wages at which they operate; no inflationary pressures are
expected, and price stability is allowed to set in. According to
the Phillips curve, any attempt to lower the unemployment rate
further would raise the inflation rate; one simple interpretation
is that low unemployment raises conflicts over wages (as wage
earners would feel less insecure about the risk of being unemployed), and wage pressures eventually lead the firms to raise
their prices. Now suppose that the government wishes to stabilize the economy at a lower rate of unemployment, and
assume that, through subtle economic policies, the government
succeeds in bringing unemployment below the natural rate of
unemployment. According to the Phillips curve, this will be at
the cost of positive inflation. For those Keynesians who would
argue that inflation matters less than unemployment, this is a
price worth paying. The monetarists would counter not by
proving that inflation is more costly than it seems but by
showing that this inflation rate is not sustainable. According to
Friedman, indeed, the effects of a sustained inflation will have
to spread to the whole economy in such a way that, before
long, contracts of all kinds will be indexed to the newly generated inflation. Friedman then asks: Once it has been taken into
account by all economic agents, who would doubt that this
newly generated inflation will lose its effect, with the result that
macroeconomic aggregates (particularly the rate of unemployment) will go back to the level that had previously been reached
without inflation?

Robert Lucas,[2] the new guru of what was to call itself the
"New Classical School," later presented this problem as follows: Nobody expects any economic effects from a monetary
reform that consists of transforming 100 old francs into one

new franc. How does inflation differ from monetary reform? In only one way: Monetary reform is an injunction that is immediately intelligible. By uttering "one" instead of "one hundred," agents take the reform for what it is: a matter of names, devoid of economic content. Pure inflation (that is, inflation without its associated redistribution effects) should be governed by the same logic. If, instead of each agent's having 100 francs available to complete transactions, agents together have 1000 francs, they simply have to multiply prices by 10 to return automatically to the initial situation. If this is not what happens, it is only because inflation is rarely as obvious as a monetary reform. It is not immediately comprehensible, and its effects are felt only over time. Only the illusion of additional wealth (all agents' simultaneously having the impression that they are earning more money) will have economic effects.

The real controversy between Keynesians and post-monetarists begins at the next stage. Keynesians believe it is probably true that only money illusion accounts for the "Phillips curve"—that is, for the possibility of bringing unemployment down below the natural rate of unemployment *thanks to* additional inflation. But examples abound to show that this illusion has played an active role. Money illusion, even it is no more than that, does exist, and it makes inflation appear effectual. For example, when it comes to interest rates, there is no doubt that a lax monetary policy makes for low real (i.e., corrected for inflation) rates. Inversely, it can be said that the disinflation of the 1980s was responsible for a rise in real rates that was so devastating to public debts.

The New Classical School does not deny that money illusion is possible and that it has been observed in the past; it denies that this illusion can be pulled out of its historical context and used as policy. It is one thing to observe that money illusion has played an active role (because agents were caught by "surprise"). It is another thing, for reasons stated by Friedman, to transform this after-the-fact realization into a recommendation for economic policy: such a recommendation is in itself a "warning" to agents, and it carries its own germs of destruction. As soon as it is understood, inflation becomes "monetary reform" again: it has no economic content. One must then lose faith in the possibility of deviating from the natural rate of unemployment for a long time.

In other words, according to the New Classical School, a Keynesian theorist whose advice is directed at governments operates without thinking of his own position—without thinking that his recommendations, once they are understood by the public, will defeat themselves, turning inflation into simple monetary reform. The New Classical School therefore claims that Keynesianism can be operational in practice (when it takes an agent "by surprise") but cannot be sustained for very long. And, furthermore, could a democratic regime use it, if it has to hide what it does in order to be efficient?

Rules and Discretion

But the New Classical School's critique goes beyond showing that no inflation can bring a sustainable supplement of growth to the economy. It wants to show that the risk a government will be tempted by the lure of inflation to take can by itself generate inflation even before the government makes it a reality. Assume, indeed, that the agents are convinced that the government will speed up inflation over the next year. Even before this inflation materializes, the agents will want to protect themselves against it. They will immediately ask for higher nominal wages and higher rents precisely in order to not be taken by surprise by government policies. If the government then acts *after* inflation expectations have been incorporated into the economy, it no longer has any choice but to accept it. But one then has the worst of all worlds: inflation without growth.

As we can see, the critique of Keynesianism by the New Classical School shows that governments are not in the same kind of relationship with the rest of society as, say, an engineer is with nature. An engineer can plan to blow up a bridge at noon without having to fear that the bridge may start shaking one minute before noon. Economic policy, on the other hand, must have such fears. Private agents, if forewarned about the intentions of governments, modify their behaviors and foil the actions of economic policy. This interaction between the present and the future is, in a sense, characteristic of the social sciences: unlike other sciences, they deal with objects whose current reality depends upon their future.

Accumulation and Expropriation

Many instances other than inflation show the scope of this analysis. In order to convey an idea of it, let me first analyze another instance: the remuneration of patents. It is rather natural that inventors be remunerated and their discoveries protected. Otherwise, what economic incentive would exist for their activities? However, it is also natural that there be a limit to the protection given them. A world in which rights continued to be granted to the inventors of the wheel, the printing press, the steam engine, and the light bulb would very soon be stifled by the fees to be paid. It is essential that simple and well-understood rules prevail in this area. Inventions most be protected appropriately, but not forever.

However, any remuneration for a *past* invention, no matter how recent, is in itself an inefficiency that the economic system would like to avoid. Any inventor living on royalties originating from his patents is a parasite. He no longer produces anything, but he forces producers to pay for what should be (and will sooner or later become) a public good. If they could, governments would like to expropriate all past rights but, at the same time, guarantee that future rights will always be protected. This has been called the "dynamic inconsistency" of the choices of governments.[3] Every government would like to be able to institute new, irrevocable policies that would abolish the past with one hand and commit to protecting the future with the other. Every government would like to call the bluff of previous policies and expropriate past inventions but, at the same time, be assured that its successors will not call their own policy's bluff (and will try to guarantee that, starting today, patents will be protected).

This metaphor about patents can easily be extended to the accumulation of capital in general. Every capitalist living on private income is also a parasite—a rentier, as Keynes would say. The fact that rentiers provided the resources for capital accumulation and for an increase in the productive forces of a country does not make any difference. Just as in the case of the inventor of the wheel, a capitalist's fate is continuously threatened by the possibility that society will choose to expropriate him. Just as in the case of patents, the only economic reason that prevents society or its government from doing so is that it might dissuade rentiers-to-be—in other words, today's savers. Expropriating the owners of capital that is already in place would not have worse economic consequences than the nonpayment of rights to the inventor of the wheel. But it is a dangerous operation because it threatens future accumulation of capital (i.e. investments). Who would choose to accumulate capital in a society that expropriates it? It is not enough to say, as Keynes did, that rentiers are parasites. They are, but so are about to be all current investors.

Tie Government's Hands . . .

Governments daily make Saint Augustine's prayer ("Give me chastity and continence, but not just now") their own. However, by postponing abstinence they may simply make its implementation harder. Once the private agents are convinced that today will always be different from tomorrow in the eye of a current government, they stop trusting that government. Thus, the monetarist critique of Keynesian policies can be interpreted as a critique of the "lack of will" of governments that postpone refraining from intervening for the reason that it is not harmful today to do so. In the absence of rules, governments will act day after day as they believe is best, and eventually ruin their credibility. Investors will not want to risk being taxed and will not accumulate capital, inventors will stop discovering ideas, inflation will build up before the fact, and the whole fabric of society will collapse.

One then sees why it is important to convince people *before the fact* that the government will not step in. Otherwise, a vicious circle of interventionism would get started—one in which a government would trail behind private agents, without even getting any benefits from its actions. To some extent, one wants to tie government's hands so as to make sure (and to convince society) that it will not intervene in the future. When it comes to inflation (which was the starting point of the analysis), nothing would better achieve this end, according to monetarists, than an independent central bank whose sole mandate would be to fight inflation and which would be independent enough to oppose, if necessary, governments that might be tempted by the inflation devil. This debate played a fundamental part in the Maastricht Treaty.

. . . and Give Government Some Discretion

For the monetarists, the outcome of the debate about "rules" versus "discretion," as Kydland and Prescott call it, leads to the defense of any procedure that restricts the government's actions in advance and subjects it to intangible rules: give the management of monetary policy to an independent central bank and forget inflation. But the debate also highlights the benefits of keeping some discretion in the hands of the government. It does not harm, in itself, to make a bonfire of past debts, and it could prove to be an excellent way of getting out of a crisis, if only one could convince the private agents that this corresponds to exceptional circumstances which are unlikely to be repeated. Keynes's suggestion that war debts be forgiven, for instance, resulted from a realistic analysis of the constraints to which governments are subject and from the implicit idea that wars are unlikely events. He was proclaiming the end of an era and calling for the establishment of another one (to which Beveridge would give content). Some would say, as the New Classical School does, that such a policy cannot constitute a solid base for economic policy. But is that enough of a reason to totally reject it? Respecting the property of rentiers because investment should not be discouraged differs very much, for example, from paying cauliflower growers a "fair" price to encourage them to produce today. Cauliflowers immediately react to prices. Capital, on the other hand, is there, intangible, whatever its price. There is not a "fair" price, as such, for capital. In Marx's language, it is dead labor. Capital is not a commodity like any other whose price results from the equilibrium between supply and demand. Whether one pays for it or not, it is already there. Think, for example, of a rental building. The building would not disappear if renters refused to pay. Only in the long run would hallways deteriorate and require new investment for proper maintenance. In the meantime, rent control is good for renters, and therefore possibly for the majority of inhabitants in a city if landlords are a minority there. Likewise, the fight against inflation, once it is won, is inevitably in danger of losing some of its intensity. Even if lax monetary policies inevitably risk a return of inflation, how can one be convinced today that they should be rejected if today they allow the abolition of unproductive income? Now that rents, wages, contracts, and debts are set up in terms that contain the agents' new non-inflationary expectations, it is possible again (which does not mean always desirable) to lower rates and stimulate activity by means of more flexible policies than those that were needed to lower inflation. How should one trade off this contradiction?

Arguments against Rules: The Debt of Developing Countries

The crisis caused by the debt of developing countries perfectly illustrates how difficult it is to manage a system in the absence of discretionary powers. According to some commentators, this crisis may have set back debtor countries more than 20 years. Many problems would have been avoided, and few costs incurred, if these debts had been thrown into a bonfire in the early 1980s.[4]

A crucial factor in the developing countries' debt crisis must immediately be pointed out: The fundamental shift that triggered the debt crisis occurred during a single period, 1980–1983. In spite of significant transfers (the recycling of petrodollars) that took place during the 1970s, the debt remained at levels that (as percentages of income) would today be regarded as extremely reasonable. The reason for the shift in the early 1980s was the same as the one we already encountered regarding the welfare state. Interest rates remained below the growth rates of the debtor economies throughout the 1970s. Consequently, the debtor countries had, in a way, been able to draw wealth from the creditor countries without any cost, just as redistributive retirement systems allow the transfer of wealth between generations at no cost to any of the generations concerned. When the interest rates shot up above the growth rates, the same mechanism that had appeared so reassuring in the 1970s (lend the excess savings of the world to the needy) became a time bomb in the 1980s. The growth of debt (led by high interest rates) soon blew out the solvency of the debtors (driven by their lower income growth rates). It took less than 3 years for this inversion of the rate hierarchy to precipitate a fatal surge in the debt. The only debtor country in the 1980s that was able to escape the debt crisis was South Korea, which immediately (as early as 1980) chose to stabilize its debt and was thus able to avoid the fatal set of circumstances in which the other debtors were caught. *Lesson 1: The developing countries' debt crisis is one of the modalities of the insolvency crisis of the welfare state.*

The International Monetary Fund played a major role in managing the crisis. During the summer of 1982 it was instrumental in avoiding a bank panic by obtaining support from the U.S. Federal Reserve which allowed banks to spread out payments for the defaulting Mexican loans. This action by the IMF (an institution created immediately after World War II, along with the World Bank) was interpreted by some as a sign that the contemporary world had become more efficient than the world of the interwar years. Historians who have studied the interwar debt crisis (which raged in Latin America in particular) have reached radically different conclusions.[5] In the 1930s, just as in the 1980s, creditors promptly constituted a council which coordinated negotiations between debtors and creditors. Consequently, creditors were able to turn to an efficient negotiating body, just as happened in the 1980s with the "steering committee" constituted by commercial banks.

On the other hand, no institution comparable to the International Monetary Fund was able in the 1930s to make the application of potential agreements contingent on the adjustment efforts of the debtor countries. Thus, there was "progress" in the 1980s as compared to the 1930s. But if one is to judge a book by its cover, one should note that in each case the negotiations lasted more than ten years. The interwar debt crisis started in the early 1930s. The first agreement aiming at "definitely" consolidating the debt was signed by Ecuador in 1941; it was followed by agreements with Brazil, Chile, and Peru. In the second case (the 1980s), the first agreement was signed by Mexico in 1990. A comparison of the agreements concluded in each period shows the two crises to have been extraordinarily parallel. Brazil, for example, offered two options to its creditors in 1943. In one case creditors would keep the principal, but the proposed interest rates would be reduced by half. In the other case creditors would receive an immediate payment corresponding to 10 percent of the debt, but both the principal and the interest would be reduced. Under the agreement signed by Mexico in 1990, either creditors would agree to lose 35 percent of their capital or the principal would be spared and interest rates would be reduced by more than one-third. (No serious consideration was given to a third option in which creditors would spread out payments for all of their loans under unfavorable conditions.) *Lesson 2: In spite of the role of new institutions such as the IMF and World Bank, it takes a long time to resolve a financial crisis between nations. It ends in a partial moratorium, but not until after a decade-long crisis.*

It would be wrong to think that debtors simply repudiated their debts and left their creditors without recourse. In some cases creditors succeeded in recovering a significant portion of their assets. Why did countries pay off a portion of their debts rather than simply repudiating them? Probably because repudiating them has some disadvantages. First of all, it means losing access to commercial loans, which makes the country in question very vulnerable because it puts it at the mercy of any liquidity crisis for its procurement of imports. While it is difficult to give an exact figure for the cost resulting from this disadvantage, an educated guess is—at the most—from 10 to 15 percent of a country's imports. This rough estimate was not picked at random; it corresponds to the percentage that debtors were willing to grant their creditors. Thus, there is no mystery to partial payment; it only highlights the fact that we are talking about very small amounts. The flow of payments expressed as a percentage of GNP never amounts to more than 15 percent of imports—that is, 3 percent of a country's GDP, whether the payments are inflows (as in the 1970s) or outflows (as in the 1980s). When these figures are compared to the transfers granted by the former West Germany to the former East Germany (with volumes exceeding 50 percent of East Germany's GDP), it becomes obvious that the debt market is really extremely small. *Lesson 3: Transfers of wealth from one country to another are extremely limited in both directions.*

A Comparison with the Savings-and-Loan Crisis

Let us now compare the debt crisis of developing countries with the savings-and-loan crisis in the United States. American savings-and-loan institutions had accumulated losses throughout the 1980s as a result of their loans to the real-estate market. When the scandal broke out, the tally of losses had an impressive magnitude: approximately $500 billion worth of debt was expected to be rescheduled (the final bill was lower). This magnitude is very close (relatively speaking) to that of the debt crisis in the developing countries. But in terms of the time it took to resolve the crisis, the differences are spectacular. This savings-and-loan crisis broke out publicly in the early part of 1988. As soon as he took office, in January 1989, President George Bush worked out an agreement with Congress. Losses were taken over by the government in their entirety, despite the enormous budget deficit. At the end of 1989 the crisis was resolved. *Lesson 4: Within a nation-state, large transfers of resources can occur which guarantee* ex post facto *that the government will intervene in a discretionary fashion to protect the population from unexpected crises.*

Rules and Discretion Reconsidered

The American government thus chose to go against any previous rules and exonerate the losses accumulated by the savings-and-loan institutions. This policy of shared losses is a sensible discretionary choice. It obliterates the debts of a bankrupt institution, discards the risk that the crisis would spread to other sectors, and transfers the burden of the debt onto society at large through taxation. These were "exceptional circumstances," and other financial institutions should obviously refrain from thinking that such circumstances might turn into an operating rule.

In the case of the debt of developing countries, on the other hand, no institution had the legitimacy needed to spread losses across society. It proves *ad absurdum* the benefit of having a legitimate government that can rapidly forgive debts.

As we know, the Bible expects debts to be forgiven every 50 years. But we also know that this injunction, if taken literally, would not be very favorable to the accumulation of capital. What is needed is a government that can forgive debts when circumstances require it—that is to say, when an unexpected set of circumstances stands in the way of the smooth functioning of the system. The problem here is that obviously these exceptional circumstances cannot become the rule, or else the New Classical School's critique would become relevant: agents would integrate the new rule in their calculations, and if every loan was guaranteed by the government the credit system would soon collapse.

How can one bring about this kind of alchemy, which gives absolute discretionary powers to the government but which, most of the time, keeps it from using them? The problem (if not its solution) can be expressed in one word: *legitimacy,* which makes it acceptable for the government to break certain rules which it otherwise has the duty to impose. Let us reassess this question through a different example: the case of Europe, which is looking for such legitimacy.

Arguments in Favor of Rules: Europe

In 1993 Europe adopted the Maastricht treaty, which aims to lay the foundations of a new Europe, able to stand on its own both as an economic power and as a military and diplomatic power. The key economic innovation of this treaty was to schedule for 1999 (at the latest) a single currency for Europe, which would be issued by an independent European Central Bank, one essentially designed on the model of the Bundesbank. This means that the European Central Bank will be independent of governments, and that it will be assigned one only goal: to guarantee price stability, paying no attention to unemployment. In terms of the monetarist debate over the (mis-) use of the Phillips curve, this is clearly a victory for Friedman's critique of Keynesian economics. Is it a good thing to have the monetarist orthodoxy imposed on the future European Central Bank, or should the long-term effects of an independent central bank be distrusted? In terms of the debate just presented, it comes down to deciding whether to set up imperative rules that stand in the way of Europe's discretionary choices or to allow for the occasional breaking of these rules.

In this respect, the difficulties associated with the construction of the new Europe bear some resemblance to the failures experienced by members of the international community in their attempts to resolve the debt crisis. Europe, no more than the IMF, has the legitimacy that would allow it to transfer the losses of one group of agents to another group. Such discretionary powers are unique to nation-states; the European Union is not one.

This realization has given rise to two radically different approaches. One approach concludes that the construction of the European Union is going astray when it arranges for transfers of sovereignty (especially in the monetary area) from the nation-states to the Community. The other approach advocates the opposite: that the construction of a European nation-state is a historical necessity that has to be started one way or another, currency being an excellent choice.

However, a decision has to be made. Is Europe bound to stay a cooperative agreement among sovereign states, or is it on its way to becoming a nation-state? If Europe wants to become a nation-state, then one should argue against rigid rules imposed on the European economic institutions, as evidenced by the example of the developing countries' debt crisis. If instead Europe is bound to remain a galaxy of nation-states which want to cohabit efficiently, then it becomes understandable that the rules of the game (a single market and possibly a single currency) should be made rigid and be excluded (as far as possible) from political renegotiation. The crisis of the European monetary system in the summer of 1993 showed how difficult it is to keep a rigid grid of parties when it is left to investors to guess what they think governments should do in the future. On the other hand, if one wants to tie a sovereign government's hands, it needs to be shown that sovereign nation-states that accept such rules can maintain the degree of freedom necessary for the exercise of their sovereignty. This second possibility is the one I would like to defend here.[6] Indeed, if we are willing to stop referring to the constitution of a European nation, it becomes much easier to interpret the European construct; it also becomes possible to justify the monetary unification of Europe without regarding it as a political construct or working toward such a goal.

A Cooperative Approach to the European Currency

An independent central bank clearly deprives governments of certain attributes of their sovereignty. In one single currency area, they will not be able to devalue or to choose their inflation rate. At least in the short run, this amounts to the loss of a policy instrument, the nature of which was analyzed above in the discussion of the Phillips curve. The disadvantage of thus losing one instrument must, however, be weighed against the benefits of a single currency in coordinating the actions of governments. Central banks and governments are now playing a game that leads them to a form of competition between nation-states. When the economy is in an inflationary cycle, each of them tries to raise its interest rates a little higher than its neighbors in order to defend its currency. This causes a useless upward bias in interest rates which is detrimental to all. In a similar (but opposite) way, downturns lead every country to try devaluating its currency against its neighbors' currencies; Europe tried to do so in the 1930s and experienced an enormous surge in protectionism that caused the collapse of international trade. An agreement in favor of a central bank can therefore be totally justified by the need for strong coordination of monetary policies in Europe, ruling out the possibility that countries can abruptly change the rules of the commercial game through "wild" devaluations.

However, the independence of the European Central Bank causes fear. The Germans are afraid that it will be subject to political pressures by member states (the French, for instance, keep saying that the ECB will enable them to regain monetary decision-making power). Others think that, on the contrary, the ECB will deprive nation-states of an attribute that is essential to national sovereignty, one not justified by the cooperative gain just outlined. Obviously the independence of a central bank is a matter of degree that has to be judged with time and will depend upon its members. It is nevertheless clear that the ECB is bound to display an intransigent attitude toward the specific needs of each nation-state. When confronting the specific disequilibria that may affect member states, the ECB will most likely be of little help to a troubled nation. This issue takes us to the core of the debate over Europe: How much latitude will the nation-states have in an integrated European Monetary Union?

Asymmetries and Fiscal Policies within Europe

The arguments in favor of the European Monetary Union (EMU) were made during the first half of the 1980s, when European countries seemed to be undergoing symmetrical shocks of an essentially external nature: oil crises, and fluctuations of the dollar and the international interest rates. The idea of a coordinated European response and even—later on—European monetary integration seemed natural at that time. Europe felt the need to respond the fluctuations of the dollar cooperatively, and so to have one currency of its own.

Today Europe is confronted with asymmetric shocks. Germany is suffering from the inflationary effects of reunification, Italy from its public deficit, and France from persistent unemployment. Each problem is specific to a particular country and requires a response tailored to it. It is fairly clear that a single currency can serve a useful purpose if all countries adhering to it are confronted with disequilibria of the same nature; however, it is obviously of much less interest if each country has its own specific problem. Fixed exchange rates and a single currency are not the best responses to asymmetric shocks.

Does this mean, however, that a persistent loss of competitiveness in one European country (in relation to others) could not be averted if a single currency were to make devaluation impossible? In addressing this question, one cannot avoid discussing fiscal policy, the other key instrument for dealing promptly with a loss of competitiveness. Indeed, there are few things that can be achieved through monetary policies that cannot also be achieved through fiscal policy. For example, a loss of competitiveness can always be offset by modifying the taxation of firms. Cancelling aid to families in France starting tomorrow would immediately result in the equivalent of a 7 percent real devaluation. The problem is that such a measure needs to be ratified by public opinion and the parliament, whereas devaluation usually occurs outside the sphere of political negotiation. Are the European democracies strong enough to do transparently what could (sometimes) be done in an opaque manner through monetary policy? This is one of the crucial issues raised by the EMU. One has the right to be doubtful, but if so it is not reasonable to oppose the EMU in the name of democracy or of sovereignty of the people (as so many politicians who fought against the Maastricht treaty have done).

Regions and Nations

A related criticism of the EMU challenges the view of the role of autonomous fiscal policies just mentioned. According to this criticism, the EMU is bound to fail in the absence of a U.S.-style federal budget, which would help Europe cope with monetary integration. It is useful to take here, as a point of departure for our analysis, some of the criticisms of the European monetary unification recently expressed by renowned economists.

Martin Feldstein (a Harvard professor and former head of Ronald Reagan's Council of Economic Advisers) published a rather harsh article opposing the Maastricht Treaty in *The Economist* (June 13, 1992), observing that the EMU will speed up the formation of a federal Europe that it will have to leave aside some of its members, thus making Europe perhaps more divided at the end of the process than it was at the beginning. A group of approximately sixty German economists (Schiller, Giersch, Neumann, Watrin, Vaubel, et al.) published an even more scathing manifesto against the European Monetary Union in which they claimed that monetary union will create economic tensions that it might lead to political conflicts which could break Europe apart rather than integrating it. These

criticisms are influenced by their authors' political and economic environments. Martin Feldstein is thinking of the American economy, and the German economists are probably
thinking of German unification. How should we interpret the
differences between regions within a national economy, and
between nations within the world economy?

Regions within a nation are often regarded as a model of
what would become of Europe under the effect of the monetary
union: limited local sovereignty, control by strong supra-
national sovereignty, and very strong economic dependence on
the "national" (i.e. supra-regional) economy. In fact, regions
within a nation are more specialized than nations within the
world economy. Rust belts and sun belts are each highly specialized, making each of these regions vulnerable to the downturns of their trade. Such specialization accounts for the harsher
nature of their overall economic situation. It is not a rare
phenomenon to see regions become poorer and depopulated for
the benefit of some of their neighbors. Pierre Mendès-France,
the courageous French politician who signed the peace treaty
between France and Vietnam in 1953, opposed the European
Common Market in 1957 precisely because of the risk that
certain regions (and consequently certain nations within
Europe) would become proportionately poorer than others.
The famous Italian economist Corrado Gini used the same
argument in the 1930s to prove the superiority of national
self-sufficiency over international trade! Although these fears
have not materialized, the danger is real. It is this kind of
destructive process, operating in East Germany, that might
explain why German economists have been so concerned about
monetary integration. Feldstein's idea is similar; according to
him, the risk of greater vulnerability for European regions

within the EMU is what would necessarily lead Europe to undertake the formation of a federal nation-state on the U.S. model.

However, there is much less labor mobility in Europe than in the United States, where a worker will typically move to another region within a year if he or she must do to find another job.[7] There is practically no way for the various states in the U.S. to stop these movements of the labor force. This mobility forces the states to exert budgetary caution, since their tax bases can be very erratic. Consequently, it is almost impossible for them to fight efficiently the economic difficulties encountered in their regions. But in Europe it is not reasonable to fear that the entire labor force will end up in a single region and that the others will become depopulated. Mobility is essentially limited to migration within the various nations. Will the EMU and the single market accelerate labor mobility? It is doubtful. The Common Market did not do so. If anything, economic theory shows that labor mobility becomes less necessary when there is free trade of goods. Thus, there are few reasons to think that economic integration will increase mobility, which is extremely limited at present. Should that happen, however, the political (and not only economic) issue would be radically modified, since a high degree of mobility of individuals might contribute to making the reference to a European "nation" more relevant. One reason why people who live in New York can consider themselves as belonging to the same nation as people who live in Los Angeles is that they can potentially live in either of these two cities. If Europeans were to regard Rome or London as two equally likely places for them (or their children) to live, then perhaps something like a European nation could emerge. Until that moment, nations within Europe will never look like regions within a nation.

Any reference to reunified Germany or the United States therefore seems inappropriate for Europe. The fears expressed by Feldstein or the German economists (according to whom European integration will disrupt the lives of Europeans in the same manner as the life of someone living in Sicily is affected by Tuscany) are farfetched.

Summary

I do not share the pessimism of those who see European monetary unification as a factor in economic and political destabilization. However, I do not share the optimism of those who see it as a panacea. The EMU appears in a new light as soon as the idea that Europe might replace the exercise of national sovereignty is left behind. On the whole, I think that, far from weakening democracy in Europe, the EMU will make its exercise more rigorous and more necessary. As I have tried to show, the success of Europe will first depend on the capacity of national democracies to respond to new imperatives which the EMU will help to define. Contrary to some of the fears expressed, the EMU should not lead to a weakening of the key instrument of national sovereignty, fiscal policy, for an essential reason that goes to the heart of why there is no European nation: the lack of labor mobility across European states. Only the nation-states have the legitimacy to tax and redistribute wealth. Europe, so far and in the foreseeable future, cannot replace the delicate balance between rules and discretion, for which only nation-states can be responsible. It is therefore natural that European institutions should not be given discretionary powers and—if a single currency is desired as a means of enhancing the collective rationality of the various European states—that the European Central Bank issuing it should be independent.

Conclusion

It is a delicate exercise to arbitrate between the choice of a "rigorous" policy (or one that respects the rules of the market) and the operation of a more interventionist policy. It is just as absurd to want to restrict a nation-state by means of intangible rules as it is to discredit the idea that those rules are necessary. No miraculous remedy exists in this area. Only an implicit contract of a political nature between a government and society makes it possible to subject the exercise of government to rules and allow it to break them if need be. Analyzing the debt of savings-and-loan institutions in the United States in relation to the debt of developing countries provides good evidence of this contradictory necessity.

However, while a crisis such as the one caused by the debt of the S&Ls reveals the nature of the problem, it fails to show the extent of it. Beyond "exceptional circumstances" justifying discretionary action, there are periods during which a government is more interventionist than it is at other times. A comparison of the 1960s with the 1980s provides good evidence of this. We have to understand the nature of such alternations in order to assess how likely it is that the "laissez-faire" of the 1980s will disappear, or whether in the years to come it will operate with the same intensity as in the 1980s.

5

Economic and Political Cycles

The first Keynes we encountered was the one who advocated the euthanasia of rentiers and who wanted to oppose "the morals, the politics, the literature, and the religion of the age," which had "joined in a grand conspiracy for the promotion of saving." The success of Keynesianism was due not only to what could be called its economic efficiency, but also to what must be called the 1960s: a state of mind favorable to opening new frontiers of solidarity. The 1980s were the reverse image of those years, and the "conservative revolution" stopped the welfare state in its tracks. From this point of view the conservative revolution may be simply interpreted as a braking mechanism which reflected the need to impose a budget constraint on government. We saw in chapter 3 how such government budget constraints resulted from the slowdown of growth below the interest rates. But there is apparently more to it than the simple mechanics of tight budget constraints: something, more psychological, of a new individualism emerged. The middle class in the United States got tired of helping the poor (as Krugman put it), people in Milan tired of helping people in Rome, and so on. These examples bear the stamp of the 1980s: a rejection of the solidarity of the 1960s, which reflected a change of mood as much as a budgetary necessity. Should this new climate be regarded as permanent? Although the slow-down of growth clearly plays a crucial role, what I want to suggest now is that the discrepancy between actual growth and expectations (rather than the level of growth itself) might actually be the key factor behind the change of political mood. From that perspective, one might conjecture that even in the absence of a return to the rapid growth of the postwar period, a mere resumption of growth beyond the low point where people are now expecting it might yield a resumption of the optimism of the 1960s. In order to consider that point, let us return to the articulation of economic and political cycles, so as to see whether we should visualize the first years of the next century as a continuation of the 1980s or as a breaking away from them.

Theories of Political Cycles

Let us first examine the way in which economists have accounted for the articulation of political and economic cycles. Today's current theories are characterized by two major trends of thought. The first school stresses the opportunism of political parties, describing them as power machines whose main objective is to be elected or reelected.[1] The second school stresses politicians' "partisan choices" and explains political cycles in terms of the intrinsic preferences of various political parties, some of which may stress efficiency and others equity.[2]

On the view of the first school, political parties simply want to maximize their chances of being (re)elected and tend to present similar programs: they vie for the center of the political spectrum in their quest for the support of middle-of-the-road voters. However, this theory needs a complement in order to account for political *cycles*. As Rogoff and Sibert explain, the alternation of parties in government is due to the voters' "disenchantment" with the present leaders.[3] This is surely a compelling description of the political cycles, and many examples come to mind that account for these switches of preferences. However, if a change in leadership were the only issue, why would politicians' ideology fluctuate to such an extent? If it were a matter of politicians' trying to imitate their voters' preferences, we would have to conclude that voters change their minds for reasons that are beyond economic reasoning—which would not make for a very powerful theory.

The other way to account for political cycles is based on the idea that political parties have intrinsically different ideological preferences. It can be said, for example, that when the left comes to power it carries out a program with strong redistribution effects in favor of the poor, whereas the right wants to emancipate the market from government control and foster economic efficiency. According to this approach, political parties do not examine in detail what voters want; on the contrary, it is for the voters to scrutinize what the parties offer. One could say, along these lines, that Americans discovered the "conservative revolution" by electing Reagan, rather than voting for it as such. It is obviously just as unsatisfactory to regard party ideology as an exogenous process as it is to claim (in the opportunistic theory) that voters' preferences are simply volatile. Among many counterexamples to the view that parties have rigid dogmas, one could note that in France the Socialist Party came to power in the 1980s, in times of conservatism, and was quick (too quick, according to pundits) to turn its policy around accordingly. Party ideology, however important it might be, is not entirely rigid.

Empirical Evidence

Beyond these questions of endogeneity of preferences, how can one empirically decide between these two approaches? There is a rather simple test. If politicians are guided by essentially voter-directed choices, there will be serious maneuvering in economic policy just before elections (in order to convince voters that the current government is effective). If, on the other hand, politicians are moved by partisan choices, the opposite occurs: economic policy actions are concentrated early in the term (because, as soon as they are elected, politicians are eager to carry out their programs).

In order to decide between the two approaches, let us examine a table set up by Alberto Alesina, who systematically explored this issue.[4] Table 5.1 highlights several fascinating dimensions of the American political economic cycle. First of all, we can see that, apart from two exceptions (marked with asterisks), every postwar recession (negative growth) broke out during the second year of a Republican mandate. This actually also holds true, historically speaking, for the years before World War II. The two postwar exceptions can be identified rather easily; they are the two oil shocks. The second important phenomenon concerns the means observed. It should be noted that economic growth in the last two years of a term is essentially the same for a Democratic or a Republican president; the sharpest contrast occurs during the first two years, with a definite advantage for the Democrats. If inflation were analyzed, the hierarchy would be reversed; on average, Republicans (over the course of a presidential term) do much better than Democrats. The conclusion Alesina draws from this table goes in the direction of "partisan" theories of political cycles. If we agree that Republicans have intrinsically more conservative preferences than Democrats, we should not be surprised to see

Table 5.1
Growth rate of U.S. GDP (for different years of the corresponding
President's term). Source: Alberto Alesina, "Macroeconomics and
politics," in *NBER Macroeconomics Annual 1988*.

	Year			
	1	2	3	4
Democrats				
Truman	0.0	8.5	10.3	3.9
Kennedy/Johnson	2.6	5.3	4.1	-5.3
Johnson	5.8	5.8	2.9	-4.1
Carter	4.7	5.3	2.5	–0.2*
Democratic mean	4.8		4.1	
Republicans				
Eisenhower 1	4.0	–1.3	5.6	2.1
Eisenhower 2	1.7	–0.8	5.8	2.2
Nixon 1	2.4	–0.3	2.8	5.0
Nixon/Ford	5.2	–0.5	–1.3*	4.9
Reagan 1	1.9	–2.5	3.6	6.4
Republican mean	1.0		3.7	

*exception

that the priority given to the fight against inflation (rather than
the fight against unemployment, which characterizes Democrats) is always accompanied by an initial tightening, which
brings about a recession. Aside from the two oil shocks, it
shows that the *single* cause of postwar recessions is the Republicans' desire to make the economy "healthier." Inversely, if
Democrats were more opportunistic and less prone to ideology,
they would try to boost the economy late in their terms rather
than early. Differences between Republicans and Democrats
seem to vanish towards the ends of their terms: growth rates
are no longer different (even though Democrats usually bring

greater inflation, due to their attempt to boost the economy early in their terms).

There is no question that the theory of partisan choices is supported by this analysis of American political cycles; this does not mean, however, that the opportunistic theory is entirely invalid. Alesina himself shows that there is a new surge of government activity just before elections. But these pre-election efforts appear to be much less significant than post-election efforts.

The two approaches are obviously not mutually exclusive in terms of election results. The parties may be guided by voter preferences, and at the same time it may be ideologically advantageous for one party to carry out a given policy. For example, whatever efforts the left might make, the right has more of a chance to win an election when the average voter is in a "conservative state of mind." Even then, however, if voters are disappointed by the ruling conservative party, they can vote for the left, provided that the left has promised to embark on a conservative program. In order to operationalize this synthesis, however, we still have to explain why voters' preferences can change. If Alesina's analysis unquestionably shows that governments are guided by partisan ideological choices, what gives rise to those ideologies and what accounts for their alternating pattern? Why did the average voter become more conservative in the 1980s? How long will this last?

Kondratieff's Cycles

In their analyses of economic cycles over the long run, Kondratieff[5] and his interpreters discovered significant regularities in the articulation of economic and political cycles. This correlation, more than the economic cycles themselves, is my concern here. It is my opinion that these cycles show governments to be interventionist in periods of rapid growth and liberal in crisis periods. The intermittent nature of these two patterns can be seen to have been operating even within the liberal era that ushered in the nineteenth century.

Kondratieff first notes that economic activity seems to be governed by a 50-year periodicity. A 25-year growth period is, "on average," followed by a 25-year crisis period, which in turn is followed by a 25-year growth period. There have been three broad cycles of this kind since the Industrial Revolution of the late eighteenth century. The pattern is as follows, if the figures are rounded off slightly:

1787–1814: growth; 1815–1849: recession (and end of first cycle)
1850–1873: growth
1873–1896: recession (and end of second cycle)
1898–1929: growth
1929–1948: recession (and end of third cycle)
1948–1973: growth
1973–1998: recession (and, perhaps, end of fourth cycle).

Table 5.2 summarizes the inflection points obtained on the major prices which give evidence of these cycles through the period immediately following World War I.

Kondratieff was deported by Stalin in the late 1920s because his theory contradicted the Marxist theory of the law of the tendency of capitalism to decline. His chronology stops immediately after World War I, but it is difficult to resist the fascination of numbers and the temptation to extrapolate from them.

Table 5.2
Peaks and trough of raw material prices. Source: Gaston Imbert, *Des mouvements de longue durée Kondratiev* (La Pensée Universitaire, 1959).

	Peak	Trough	Peak	Trough	Peak	Trough
Coal	1814	1851	1873	1896	1929	
Steel	1801	1850– 1852	1873	1893– 1985	1929	
Cotton	1799	1845	1864	1898	1918	1933
Wheat	1812	1851	1873	1894		

Kondratieff pointed to some correlations between economic and political cycles. He noted that wars are most numerous during expansionary periods, whereas recessionary periods tend to be more favorable to peace. He also noted that revolutions often occur in transition periods, when crises are replaced by growth.

Gaston Imbert,[6] a faithful interpreter of Kondratieff who wrote immediately after World War II, gave a picture of economic cycles and corresponding social and political events before World War I that can be briefly summarized as follows.

A century before World War I, Europe was left exhausted at the end of the Napoleonic wars. The Congress of Vienna, which sealed the peace, orchestrated the revenge of political reaction. The agitation of the French Revolution was followed by a long period of conservatism. The European economy entered a long phase of deflation. The slump in prices tipped the scales of history in favor of rentiers. Becoming rich meant lending or buying perpetual rents. Those who went into debt in order to invest were brutally hit by the drop in prices. Governments were no exceptions. Their only objective seems to have been paying off the debts they had incurred during the Napoleonic wars. Budgetary and political conservatism reinforced each other and ruled until the middle of the nineteenth century.

In 1848 this movement was reversed and society underwent abrupt changes. The French King Louis Philippe was deposed, and Metternich, the Austrian master of reaction after the Napoleonic wars, fled. Gold was discovered in California and Australia. Prices were climbing; inflation favored investors. The political atmosphere changed in parallel ways. The keepers of conservative morals were booed; in the years 1848–1873, Marxism appeared and the myths of the French Revolution were rediscovered. Society was restless and discarded the keepers of orthodoxy it had chosen in the wake of the Napoleonic wars. The business world saw the arrival of a new generation of individuals who were only 10 years old in 1810 and did not have the same aversion to war as the "veterans." As a result of the rise in prices, as well as of the new generation and the financial comfort due to economic growth, governments were no longer hesitant to play a role again in directing the fate of nations. The increasing number of wars among the major nations paralleled rising prices: there were wars in Crimea and Italy, the American Civil War, wars between Prussia and Denmark, Austria and France, Austria and Italy, and a war between Prussia and France.

The intensification of wars between nation-states was paralleled by intensification in other areas. Strikes were on the rise, and so were civilian killings and burglaries. Imbert put it as follows: "More premeditated homicides, more cases of assault and battery, more crimes against society, in other words more killings and burglaries: wealth generates envy. Economic fever excites passions . . . , immorality spreads."[7]

The year 1873 marks the beginning of a downward phase in the Kondratieff cycle. Once again, the crisis would last 25 years. This period, which covers the years 1873–1898, was to be called "Great Recession" by historians. There was another reversal of the system of values. Winds of universal peace were blowing over European nations, and the few wars that still broke out were limited to peripheral areas. The crisis revived the conservative morals of small savers. To quote Imbert again: "The period of decline appears to us as strangely peaceful, as a period of political and social tranquillity. By reducing profits, economic regression brings back morals: divorces are less common, more children are born, fewer are abandoned, and the number of abortions goes down. As prices decline, the crime rate goes down, the social organism calms down."[8] The only "black spot" in the picture is that the suicide rate went up: recession brings "morality" up but seems to bring happiness down.

In 1898, the Dreyfus case was reopened and the French left stood up against the rising French anti-semitism, gold was discovered in Alaska and South Africa, and capitalism was entering its third Kondratieff growth phase since the beginning of the industrial revolution. The era of steam engines and railroads was succeeded by the era of automobiles and electricity. The joyful dance of history resumed its amnesic course. Growth was celebrated and wars resumed: the Sino-Japanese War (in 1895, somewhat ahead of time), the Spanish-American War (1898), the Boer War (1899), the Greek-Turkish War (1897), the Russian-Japanese War (1903–1904), the Italian-Turkish War (1911), the Balkans War (1912), and the conflict named "World War I" (which is the worthy heir of the Napoleonic wars and which occurred at the highest point of the growth period). This growth period was to continue for several more years after the war (as it did a century earlier) before extending into a new deflationary period, probably between 1925 and 1930.

The Theories of Cycles

The two major theories that account for these economic cycles were introduced in previous chapters. The first one is monetarist theory; it explains that the discovery of gold mines resulted in an injection of liquid assets, which boosted the economy. Today one would say—in terms of the theory of rational expectations—that it injected liquid assets "by surprise" and implicitly invalidated previous (nominal) contracts, which provided new entrepreneurs with additional resources at the expense of rentiers. The other theory, which is upheld by Schumpeter, sees waves of "creative destruction" coexisting with each of the high periods in the cycle. The first wave starts with the first industrial revolution. The second wave is associated with railroads in the 1850–1873 cycle. The third wave is associated with the second industrial revolution (electricity, chemicals, automobiles) in the 1898–1923 cycle, and the fourth with "Fordism" in the 1948–1973 cycle.

These theories can serve as a point of departure for an attempt to analyze the reasons why it is possible to imagine that a new expansionary cycle might begin in 1998. The monetarist interpretation suggests that growth could be reactivated through a new inflationary cycle, which would "take by surprise" all those who thought that the fight against inflation would go on forever. The Schumpeterian interpretation of cycles suggests that the computer revolution is still in its infancy and will induce a strong recovery once it has generalized.[9]

It would be risky to go any further in this direction. Let us only assume that the phenomena just listed have played and will play a part. Kondratieff's cycles are useful not so much in helping us forecast the economic cycle (unless we become superstitious) as in helping us understand how political cycles are generated.

War and Peace

The analysis of wars provides a fundamental clue in the analysis of regularly occurring changes in the relationship among government, society, and markets before World War II. There is no question that, as table 5.3 shows, wars preceding and including World War I broke out during the high periods of Kondratieff's cycles. In crisis periods nation-states turn in on themselves; in periods of economic expansion, on the other hand, they make war on their neighbors. What causes this positive correlation between war and prosperity, and why was it invalidated by World War II?

Most of the theories that were developed in the 1930s and the 1940s implicitly rely on a Keynesian view of economic cycles. Military expenditures are said to be good for growth because they create outlets, which is why war brings prosperity. Peace, on the other hand, is said to trigger recession: after a brief period during which reconstruction stimulates the economy, peace closes some outlets and slows down growth. Alvin Hansen, the first American Keynesian, remarked on this phenomenon and made a practical recommendation based on it: economic cycles would totally disappear if only nation-states would avoid the second phase (when they try to pay off their war debts and have to reduce their spending).[10]

However, there is more to it than this correlation. As Imbert demonstrated, a war usually begins in the *last* part of a growth cycle rather than the first part. Wars seem to be generated by growth, not the reverse. In his correlational analysis of wars

Table 5.3

Wars and Kondratieff cycles in the nineteenth century. Source: Gaston Imbert, *Des mouvements de longue durée Kondratiev* (La Pensée Universitaire, 1959).

Upward phase: 1790–1814

1792: Invasion of France

1796: Bonaparte's campaign in Italy

1798: Second campaign in Egypt

1800: Marengo

1805–1815: Napoleonic Wars

Downward phase: 1815–1849

1823: Spanish war

1828: Navarin war

1832: siege of Anvers

Upward phase: 1850–1873

1853: Crimean war

1858: Italian war

1864: Prussian-Danish war

1866: Austrian-Prussian and Italian-Austrian war

1870: French-Prussian war

Downward phase: 1874–1896

1877: Balkan war

1885: Bulgarian-Serbian war

1894: Japanese-Chinese war

Upward phase: 1896–1929

1897: Greek-Turkish war

1898: American-Spanish war

1904: Japanese-Russian war

1911: Italian-Turkish war

1912: Balkan war

1914: World War I

and the English rate of unemployment, Alec Macfie reaches the same conclusion: "Sparks . . . fly in the second stage of expansion."[11]

Many authorities similarly think that economic cycles cause wars, rather than that wars cause economic cycles. For example, according to Lenin imperialism is the supreme stage of capitalism during which wars between nation-states serve the interests of their bourgeoisies. The preparatory stages of war correspond to the times when government intervention is needed to guarantee the supply of raw materials and the protection of external markets. At the peaks of the cycles, when raw materials tend to become too expensive, states have to intervene militarily. Paul Kennedy, the author of the best-seller *The Rise and Fall of the Great Powers,*[12] can also be considered as one of the defenders of this causality. As Kennedy sees it, economic wealth permits military power. His theory of "imperial overstretch" explains the extent to which the great powers depend on their economic wealth to stay the leaders of their times, and how they are always driven to overdraw on their resources in order to defend their political power. It occurred in Spain in the sixteenth century, in England in the nineteenth century, and perhaps in the United States in the twentieth century. In each case, the state was bankrupting the economy to achieve its goals. Where Lenin saw the hand of the bourgeoisie pushing nation-states to protect their markets, Kennedy sees the reverse: nation-states wanting power and taking advantage of their bourgeoisies in order to accomplish their goals.

Lenin's idea that wars are triggered by nation-states in order to protect their bourgeoisies is surely excessive. It has been noted that in the case of World War I capitalists on both sides of the Rhine favored peace over war. Karl Polanyi shows very forcefully that nothing could be more alien to the nineteenth century than the idea that the interests of a nation-state coincide with the interests of its capitalists.[13] Thus, the picture of the governments of creditor countries taking military action and bombing the harbors of debtor countries proves to be naive. In an overwhelming majority of cases the payment of debts has at most served as a pretext.

In any case, if Lenin's theory were right, there would be as many reasons for war in recessionary periods as there are in expansionary periods: it is in recessionary periods that it becomes more urgent to protect one's markets; it is in periods of weak economic activity that competition is the strongest. Evidence for the latter point is provided by the fact that economic wars (such as those brought on by protectionism) occur more often during recessionary phases. In expansionary periods nation-states tend to practice free trade, which is a kind of economic peace. As I have noted (following Imbert), there are many more wars in expansionary periods than in periods of economic crisis. World War II, which seems to contradict this rule, is in fact a perfect illustration of it: it is rather obvious that neither England nor France wanted this war (under almost any circumstances), as is evidenced by all the hesitations of these two nations—the strongest in Europe—from 1936 to 1938. The crisis took away their desire for war. It was mankind's tragedy that Hitler was the first one to understand that.

Kennedy's implicit thesis is more convincing, and it is consistent with the fiscal history of nation-states (as summarized in appendix B below, which shows them to be constantly suffocated by the costs of war and unable to keep up with the pace of new military technologies). This is the same idea that I introduced in my analysis of the crisis of the welfare state in chapters 3 and 4: that economic growth allows government interventionism, rather than government interventionism fostering economic growth (as the Keynesians thought). Likewise, it seems reasonable to conclude that economic growth is what makes wars possible, rather than that wars cause of economic growth.

Public and Private Happiness

Kondratieff's history lesson may be difficult to interpret, but it is first and foremost a lesson in modesty. After hearing it, it is difficult to give credence to those who would like to convince us that we are living at the "historic end" of this or that. Those who, at one time or another, announced the end of capitalism, the end of socialism or of "laissez-faire," the end of wars, and the end of crises were all in error. It seems that every generation attempts to demonstrate the end of things that were conceived or realized by previous generations. (Obviously this criticism will also be directed at those who are announcing the end of "Keynesianism.")

However, this brief chronicle of economic and political cycles also sheds light on another aspect of the crisis of Keynesianism—one that is less mechanical in nature than the fiscal argument. It highlights a cycle that is as "psychological" as it is economic. This is echoed by Albert Hirschman,[14] whose analysis can be briefly summarizes as follows: People want "collective happiness" in periods of growth, when private consumer goods are plentiful and the need for "private happiness" can be satiated. But when economic expansion is weak and material goods are scarce, people are bored with "politics," or the collective good, while individual values and the pleasures of family life are praised along with the quest of private wealth. So there is a moral archetype for the "1960s" and a moral archetype for the "1980s," corresponding respectively to the years of "healthy cows" and the years of "lean cows." Marx and John Kennedy, among others, fall into the first category; Hayek and Ronald Reagan, among others, fall into the second category. The former proclaim the end of the individual; the latter make him an angel.

In Hirschman's terms, the *level* of wealth (or of the growth rate of the economy) counts less than how much wealth differs from individuals' "psychological" expectations about it. Feeling deprived of the (growth of) affluence, which they had taken for granted, agents become "individualistic." By contrast, as soon as people are happily "surprised" by a degree of affluence that goes beyond their expectations, they are much more ready to share through public actions the surplus that befalls them. Governments regain legitimacy, which allows them to challenge the distribution of wealth (since the return of prosperity takes away agents' fears that the government will make them poor). Such public actions may be of a warlike nature (the August 1914 model) or of a peaceful nature (the May 1968 model).

Another facet of the crisis of Keynesianism thus appears as a result of the time it takes for a society to adapt to weaker-than-expected growth. Although in most rich countries (especially in Europe) economic growth is unlikely to reach post-World War II levels again, it seems reasonable to say that the desire for public actions will reappear as soon as growth has exceeded the low point at which agents' expectations will have stabilized. If this moment is not too far away, we may see the end of the political cycle of the 1980s. Being less conservative, agents could adhere to a new doctrine that would give back to government the free hand that the conservative revolution took away from it. This new doctrine would argue that it was high time to engage in bold actions and, consequently, would be able to explain the useless of defending a monetary orthodoxy that only benefits rentiers. Voters, comforted by the totally subjective promise of new prosperity, would then initiate a new political cycle of a more interventionist nature.

Conclusion

The above analysis suggests that it takes more than being tired of the conservative ideology for voters to turn to another ideology. (If they are tired of conservatives, they can elect leftists who promise to practice the same policy.) For voters to make a new "partisan" choice, it also takes a sign that the times are about to change and that renewal is possible.

This promise of renewal is just as psychological as it is real. It is related to the gap between expectations and reality; "good surprises" are possible again if expectations always end up adjusting to reality. Obviously, the more difficult it is to let go of lost prosperity, the longer the adjustment period is.

How long should it take for one concept of prosperity to be totally discarded and replaced by another which would be modest enough for pleasant surprises to happen again? Kondratieff's cycles suggest a symmetry between the years of lean cows and the years of healthy cows. Assuming that it takes 25 years of (what is perceived as) misery to forget 25 years of healthy cows, we should be close to the end by this account. But who can be sure of it? Let us listen to the words of Proust: "I now felt that before I could totally forget you, just like a traveler who returns the same way to his point of origin, I would be able to regain my initial indifference only after going in reverse through all the feelings that I had experienced."[15] Let this be an augury!

6

The Two Crises of Keynesianism

The crisis of Keynesianism became obvious during the 1970s, when industrialized countries were plagued by "stagflation." A combination of stagnation and inflation was first seen as a contradiction in terms. Economists and politicians who were used to reasoning along Keynesian lines wanted to believe that only one of these two evils could be experienced at once. In the eyes of a Keynesian, there is inflation when demand (and "therefore" growth) is strong. On the contrary, there is stagnation when demand (and therefore inflationary pressure) is weak. However, as soon as both supply and demand are taken into account, stagflation becomes less mysterious. If the supply of goods becomes insufficient for the demand, there will be a price increase *and* a decrease in production. If an agricultural economy experiences a bad crop, there will be less bread *and* it will cost more.

This stagflation has given rise to two theories of the crisis. One explains why the demand is too strong, the other explains why the supply has declined.

The first is a neo-monetarist theory which shows that agents gradually immunize themselves against inflation by indexing wages and contracts. The monetarist critique accuses Keynesianism of being able to act only "by surprise," outside the transparency rules upon which a democracy is entitled to insist; most important, it accuses Keynesianism of having only temporary effects. According to this theory, the boost to the economy induced by government policies vanishes as soon as agents protect themselves against money illusion *before the fact.* Stagflation must then be interpreted as the inescapable outcome of a process in which agents learn to foil the effects of a government induced boost to the economy by indexing their wages to inflation before the fact. This theory results in a fundamental renewal of the theory of government; however, the practical conclusion to which it leads, namely setting up intangible rules for government action, might fall into oblivion when these rules look unnecessarily binding, and it is reasonable to think that, once the disinflation phase is over, governments will, for better or worse, give up their "new" monetary orthodoxy.

The second crisis of Keynesianism is much more serious. Industrialized countries, which for a long time were deluded by the idea that Keynesianism had created prosperity, are now painfully discovering that prosperity created Keynesianism and that the welfare state was only one of the modalities of the whittling away of prosperity. It now appears that the weakening of the welfare state is due to the weakening of postwar growth.

The slowdown of growth did not have the same form in the United States as in Europe. In Europe, the slowdown of growth was the end of a period of catching up to the United States (an end that may now be coming in Japan). In the United States, the productivity slowdown had more to do with an extreme deregulation of the labor market. Europeans gradually had to realize that their long-run growth cannot be expected to return to postwar levels. All the social institutions designed during the 1950s and the 1960s consequently have to be reconsidered, and this process may not have yet reached its climax. In the United States, which did not benefit from the same fast growth in the years that followed World War II, the problem is different, as key elements of the European welfare state are still missing there. To some extent one may say that the low productivity of the U.S. economy in the years that followed the first oil shock in the 1970s is a reflection of this lack of social institutions, as the unemployed had no other choice but to take low-pay, low-productivity jobs.

There are two possible attitudes regarding the redirecting of economic policies to the priorities that have become those of the "new world" of post-Keynesianism. On the "laissez-faire" view, government withdraws from the arbitrations which the slowdown in growth has made necessary and lets the market manage the new conflicts. On the "corporatist" view, government continues to take the initiative and forces the "social partners" to a collective resolution of the crisis, particularly in the area of employment. To put it bluntly, adoption of the "laissez-faire" view in Europe would lead to abolishing the minimum wage and letting the market create new areas of employment. The corporatist method would double the resources devoted to *active* measures for helping the jobless rejoin the work force, to the detriment of other beneficiaries of the welfare state.

Wondering which of these two attitudes is "better" would not advance the debate. The better one is the one that is politically acceptable.

The "laissez-faire" view was the rule in the 1980s. The societies that were best prepared for it (Anglo-Saxon societies) went along with it fully. Other societies tried it out more timidly. European social-democrat countries plunged into laissez-faire in a way that was as clumsy as the beginnings of the "war on poverty" in the United States during the 1960s. However, as a result of wanting to protect both the minimum wage and the welfare state, thus trying to maintain in a period of slower growth the institutions that had been created in a period of strong growth, European countries have reached the worst possible compromise and allowed unemployment to get out of hand.

The "corporatist" approach, which was followed in the Scandinavian countries, was another way to cope. But this approach too precipitated a crisis as the cost that it required in practice to be operational got out of hand as a result of budgetary problems. In fact, governments all over the world had to stand back—less often out of conviction than as a result of the budgetary problems that they had to suffer as a consequence of slower growth.

Beyond the unpleasant arithmetic of tight budget constraints, governments had to suffer another related (but not quite identical) crisis. Their legitimacy was eroded as their constituencies changed their mood about the amount of solidarity that a society should provide. Beyond the dynamics of slow growth, something akin to disappointment with the disparity between what individuals expected and what they received might stand behind this change of attitude. From that perspective, it might be that a renewed legitimacy of government's role will be forthcoming as people get used to their "new" standards of living.

If we then accept the idea that the political crisis of government is a temporary phenomenon, it is reasonable to think that regaining legitimacy—thanks to an overall economic situation that would finally be better than "expected"—would enable governments to impose these new arbitrations in favor of the cohesion of society (for the benefit of the poor or of the unemployed). In Europe, this might have to be done at the expense of the current beneficiaries of the welfare state (pensioners, sick people, families). Keynes's euthanasia of rentiers for the benefit of the productive forces of society would then be carried out. It will be just as difficult for this message to be heard today as it was yesterday. If it could be heard, however, it could take Europe to new socially efficient tradeoff between growth and employment. Ironically, this same swing of the pendulum might take the United States away from the laissez-faire dogma to a middle-of-the-road policy like that followed in Europe in the 1980s. This might turn out to be a bad compromise if the United States were to ignore the lessons of European unemployment.

As a matter of fact, should government indeed regain legitimacy, nothing tells us that this regained legitimacy would necessarily be used to take care of the cohesion of society at large. It is perfectly conceivable that a government would, for example, put its regained legitimacy at the service of militant neo-protectionism in order to try to defend the status quo of society—which in practice means the status quo ante. Among other things, this would have the effect of sharpening tensions between the North and the South, and possibly leading to war—it would be Hirschman's model à la August 1914.

However, it is possible that industrialized countries will choose the path of more peaceful collective happiness, learning to reintegrate the poorer segments of society and taking technological progress and international trade for what they are:

first a source of transitional disequilibria, then a source of persistent growth in wealth—Hirschman's model à la May 1968. If this were the case, the whole world might embark on the narrow path leading to the possibility of enjoying the same fate as industrialized nations: we would see a reduction of inequality throughout the world, and the history of nations would have a happy ending.

Appendix A
The History of Wealth

For a long time mankind's only economic problem has been to feed itself. And for a long time, from the creation of the world to the Neolithic period (12,000 years ago), human beings were able to feed themselves by freely taking what nature offered them. Hunting and gathering—two activities that do not require any social organization—were sufficient.

Good things always come to an end. At the Neolithic stage, the human population became too abundant with respect to the surrounding animal and plant world. Humankind discovered the need to cultivate plants and raise animals through its own efforts. This was a time when people would decide to enclose and cultivate a field and say (to parody Rousseau) "This is ours." Suddenly the capacity to feed people was multiplied by 10 or sometimes 100. The great civilizations of antiquity originated in this act of appropriating nature.

In the tenth century, country life in Europe was closed to the rest of the world because of the ongoing threats of Vikings in the north, Moslem or Magyar pillagers in the south and the east, and indigenous bandits in the center. There was almost no traffic of goods or people. As Henri Mendras states in *The Vanishing Peasant,* "Carolingian Europe was entirely rural: there were no cities, only farm regions populated by peasants grouped in villages around the manors of *seigneurs*. These lords constituted the entire surrounding society."[1] The history of the modern world begins at this point at which, in the early part of our millennium, the autarkic units of the Middle Ages fell apart, as people and goods started moving around again.[2]

In the late tenth century, Viking threats subsided; highways became passable again; the trading of goods and the movement of people could resume. The gold which had been hoarded by the Church was being exchanged for goods again, partly due to the Vikings themselves: they would steal this religiously guarded gold, then spend it. This development was paralleled by a spectacular increase in agricultural productivity. To quote Henri Mendras again: "[In the tenth century] the farmer used to fashion his own tools, most of them wooden, from the shovel to the swing plow. They provided him with a primitive and not very profitable means of cultivation; the yield of cereals was hardly more than two or three times the seed. The eleventh and twelfth centuries saw a simultaneous increase in the area of cultivated land and in peasant population. Implements grew in number and efficiency: shovels, spades and swing plows were now made of iron, and harrows came into use. The horse collar and the water mill gained acceptance. The [resulting] yields were to remain the same until the eighteenth century."

Agricultural progress allowed people to be better nourished. The death rate was going down and the birth rate up, and soon the progress of agricultural productivity was outstripped by the population growth it had induced. Overpopulation caused people to be pushed away to less fertile areas. Food became scarce. The first famines occurred as early as the beginning of the fourteenth century, making people vulnerable to disease and epidemics. The bubonic plague that hit London in the middle of the fourteenth century was not just an "addition" to famines; rather, the stage was set for it by the weakening of people's bodies. Overpopulation also brought about urban unhealthiness, which created a fertile ground for the spreading of epidemics. Famine, pestilence, and war, the three scourges that befell people in the fourteenth century, had cumulative effects—but famine was the condition that permitted the devastation brought about by the other two other. By the end of the fourteenth century, the population of Europe was down 40 percent from the highest point it had reached at the beginning of the century. It was not to reach such levels again until the early seventeenth century.

The "Renaissance," which starts in the middle of the fifteenth century, corresponds to the stage in which the agricultural iron collar disappeared and the population began to grow again. In the "broad" sixteenth century (from the middle of the fifteenth to the middle of the seventeenth century) we find the same sequence as in the eleventh and twelfth centuries. Europe, being less populated, could enjoy good agricultural productivity through concentrated efforts on the most fertile land. Agricultural surpluses allowed some people to leave the land and go to cities, where they took part in the resumption of trade. But identical causes unfortunately have identical effects: the agricultural stranglehold reappeared as soon as the population of Europe went back up to its early-fourteenth-century level. Although not as seriously as in the fourteenth century, the infernal trio of famine, pestilence, and war began to devastate Europe again. The Thirty Years' War (1618–1648) brought dysentery, typhus, smallpox, and the plague. France was hit by famine at regular intervals: between 1628 and 1638, from 1646 to 1652, in 1693–94 (when it was so serious as to be called "The Great Famine"), and in 1774–75.

According to Albert Soboul, "overall, 80 percent of the population hardly managed through strenuous work to feed 20 percent privileged individuals, bourgeois and craftsmen." And Paul Bairoch adds that "the full significance of these percentages, this 20–30 percent 'surplus,' comes to light if one takes into account a factor which is often overlooked in explanatory schemes of economic development: the yearly fluctuations of the yield of agricultural productions. Let us not forget that on the average they exceed 25 percent even at the national level. It is therefore inevitable that subsistence crises will periodically occur; they vary in intensity, but in their most acute form they can lead to the decline of economic life and occasionally the civilization it supports."[3]

The Agricultural Revolution

The French historian Le Roy Ladurie speaks of "motionless history" in characterizing the economics of the period extending from the fourteenth to the eighteenth century. Likewise, as we have seen, Henri Mendras stressed the fact that agricultural productivity had remained more or less constant during this period. Then came a turnabout from the middle of the seventeenth century to the middle of the eighteenth, when a new agricultural revolution—exported from Holland to England, then to France and the rest of Europe—improved agricultural yields dramatically.

Progress came through the diffusion of a crop-rotation system which totally eliminated fallow fields. Soil regeneration was now accomplished through the sequencing of crops that used different chemical elements of the soil at variable depths, through the introduction of plants with regenerative effects, and, most important, through the use of the manure produced by more extensive herds—which depended on the fodder crops included in the rotation.

Just as in the eleventh and twelfth centuries, the agricultural revolution improved traditional tools and equipment and introduced new ones. Plows were improved through the greater use of iron. Sickles were replaced by scythes, and seeders took the place of broadcast sowing or sowing with a draw hoe.

Next came progress in the selection of seeds and animal stock. New agricultural techniques accelerated the clearing of new arable land and the draining of marshy areas. There was also more and more use of horses in agricultural work. Since on average a horse can draw about 50 percent faster than an ox, the greater use of horses in agriculture resulted in a similar increase in productivity for a good number of tasks.

Jean-Claude Asselain sums up this overall process as follows: "Within a century (1650–1750) the introduction of new crops and new crop rotations, the gradual disappearance of fallow fields, the development of animal breeding, the development of manure, the selection of seeds and the improvement of animal stocks resulted in exceptional agricultural growth: while it occurred at a slow and almost imperceptible pace (a 0.5 percent yearly growth rate), its cumulative effects over a century represent an unprecedented 50 to 100 percent increase in productivity for each farmer and in agricultural production per capita."[4]

Quesnay and the Physiocrats

Being fascinated with the progress of the agricultural revolution, François Quesnay[5] and his followers the Physiocrats (a group of French economists writing in the middle of the eighteenth century) wanted to regard agriculture as the source of all wealth. If one reflects on the extent to which the history of human beings depends on their capacity to feed themselves, one can certainly concur that this is indeed the right emphasis.

Land, according to the Physiocrats, is a "gift of nature." It has the divine property of giving more than it takes. If ten men need ten apples to be nourished everyday, land—in its "generosity"—might well be tilled by these ten men up to the point where it delivers twelve apples daily. This surplus of two apples (or of two men) is the source of all increments to wealth—of "economic growth," to use modern language.

This divine nature requires the "right social institutions" in order to be exploited. The "modern" defense of private property is present in Quesnay's writings. Quesnay wanted "the legitimate owners of real estate and personal property to be assured of ownership, since the security of ownership is the essential foundation of a society's economic order." " Without the security of ownership," he continued, "the land would remain uncultivated."[6] While favoring the institutions that would prepare for the rise of modern capitalism, Quesnay nevertheless turned his back when it came to analyzing industry. In the Physiocrats' writings, industry does not and never will contribute to society's production of wealth. Let me briefly elucidate the way in which Quesnay and the Physiocrats "demonstrated" this second point.

Industry is the area in which competition between producers inevitably forces them to sell their goods at manufacturing cost. Were the sale price to be higher than the manufacturing cost, new producers would enter, selling at lower prices and driving others away; thus, there can never be a persistent gap between the price and the cost of an industrial commodity. To be more accurate: Industry and trade can provide wealth only if the laws of competition have been thwarted. In order to avoid this,

Quesnay wants the market to act as a "police force": ". . . full freedom of trade must be maintained, for no other policy in domestic and foreign trade can be as sound, accurate and advantageous to the nation and government as full freedom in competition." The term "laissez-faire" (let do) was invented by the Physiocrat Vincent de Gournay. By imposing competition on the "sterile" class (as Physiocrats would call industry), one ensures that this class will not become unduly wealthy and one makes sure that only food will pay a surplus. It took an industrial revolution to force the economists to reconsider the view that industry was sterile.

The Industrial Revolution

Between 1700 and 1800, output per agricultural worker rose 100 percent in England and approximately 70 percent in France. The agricultural revolution was not a uniform process. It made some people rich (those who knew how to take advantage of technological progress) and ruined others. Those who became rich were to spend their surplus in two areas: textiles (which have always been the first type of consumer good to which a society turns once it is freed of the constraint of feeding itself) and metallurgy (in line with the higher consumption of iron associated with the agricultural revolution). This led to several fundamental changes in the textile area, which were all adapted to small rural production: Hargreaves's famous "spinning Jenny" in 1765, then in 1771 Arkwright's water frame (which used water power as an engine), and finally Crompton's mule, which combined the two systems. This led to development in the energy sector. Watt's steam engine, the first model of which was completed in 1769, soon provided another source of power. Finally, great progress in metallurgy allowed the substitution of coke for charcoal in steelmaking. From then on, there would be a continuous flow of innovations. One can say, following Paul Bairoch, that the most significant event since the Neolithic period was on its way.

The Classical Writers

As they watched the transition to an industrial economy, the classical writers, from Smith to Ricardo, had to change the Physiocrats' economic view of industry as a sterile class.[7]

The starting point of the classical writers was to accept the Physiocrats' idea that competition forces the alignment of prices and costs. Like the Physiocrats, they wholeheartedly advocated "laissez-faire," the free play of competition. However, contrary to the Physiocrats, they did not measure the production of wealth on the basis of the difference between the sale price and the production cost. Rather, they took into account only the production cost. In a hunting society the "value" of a beaver is determined by the amount of time it takes a hunter to catch it, rather than the difference between this hunting cost and the sale price. A society gets rich in proportion to the *total sum* of effort. The classical writers' theory of labor value can be understood only in light of their attempt to redefine the wealth produced by a nation as a sum total of the efforts expended (rather than just the entrepreneurs' surplus).

But, then, what about the "surplus" brought by land? How should one compare industry and agriculture? According to the classical writers, the fundamental difference between industrial production and agricultural production is as follows: It is easy to increase industrial production twofold if one so desires; all it takes is building twice as many factories and hiring twice as many workers (demographics permitting, of course). Agricul-

tural production, on the other hand, faces an insurmountable obstacle, namely the scarcity of land. This "gift of nature," to use the Physiocrats' expression, is of limited size. Land rent (which measures this "gift"), far from being proof of nature's generosity, is proof of its avarice. As population keeps growing, agricultural production necessarily has to make use of land of decreasing fertility. Suppose that 100 men can produce 100 tons of grain when they cultivate the best plots of land; it may be that 200 men will produce only 150 tons if another 100 men must cultivate lower-quality land. Land rent has its origins in the declining productivity of cultivated land, the increasing lack of fertility of the land. This particular point, which was most forcefully stressed by Ricardo (although previous writers such as Turgot had already raised the issue), was the most fundamental turnabout taken by the classical school. It would lead, half a century later, to "neoclassical" analysis, which today is the dominant theory.

Ricardo's demonstration is extremely simple. If land is of uneven quality, someone who owns the best plots of land can ask to be paid a rent corresponding to the fertility value of his property. The greater the difference in fertility between the good and bad plots of land, the higher this rent will be. One therefore sees why, contrary to the Physiocrats' assertions, landowners' revenues reflect God's avarice rather than his generosity—no landowner could ever claim any rent if all plots of land were of uniformly high quality. Indeed, if landowners competed against one another and there was enough good land to feed the population, any rent claimed by a landowner would redirect agricultural production to another (cheaper) one, and so on. The principle of competition would work just as well in the agricultural area as it does in the industrial area. Whenever high-quality land is scarce, landowners can use the best plots to collect rent, which farmers simply have to pay unless they turn to plots that are cheaper but also of lower quality.

Let us, however, stick to the Physiocrats' emphasis on the agricultural bottleneck. How does the new approach of Ricardo and Malthus alter the Physiocrats' view of mankind's destiny? Is it not still the case that the number (and therefore the value, so to speak) of city dwellers is determined by the productivity of agriculture? Doesn't "economic growth" (to use an anachronism) still depend only on agricultural surplus? Despite a radically changed perspective on the "nature and causes of the wealth of nations," the classical writers remained, in many ways, locked into a logic that led them to answer these questions in the affirmative. Despite their desire to project the history of nations into the future, they were still dependent on the legacy of the past millennia.

Indeed, the classical writers' picture of the stages of economic growth does not differ in any significant manner from that of Cantillon, the precursor of the Physiocrats. Any improvement in the standard of living automatically triggers an exponential increase in population; this is Malthus's law, which was also clearly expressed by Ricardo. Given the scarcity of good land, this process causes the prices of agricultural goods to rise, increases the cost of labor, and forces capitalists to reduce their profits. There inevitably comes a time when the rise in agricultural prices stifles demographic and economic growth.

Thus, it is obvious that, in the end, the classical writers, while rejecting the Physiocrats' idea that land is the only source of wealth, adhered to the idea that industrial production is limited by "agricultural surplus." Therefore, "growth" is necessarily a transitory phenomenon, corresponding to the shift of part of the rural population to cities (or at least to industrial activities).

Marxism

Writing half a century after the classical writers, Marx could see the extensive transformation of English society that resulted from the industrial revolution. In 1846, when England decided (under Ricardo's posthumous influence) to proceed with massive imports of wheat, its agricultural population had already been reduced to 35 percent of the total population. Capitalism, which had come out of small-scale rural production, was moving to cities and creating factories. If economic growth is more than a "transition" from the countryside to cities, should one still think (as did John Stuart Mill, the last of the Classical writers, writing in the middle of the nineteenth century) that it will necessarily stop? Marx was to answer this question affirmatively, offering a demonstration that, in a way, was still inspired by the Physiocrats.

Marx takes a simple point of departure: If labor is the source of the values produced, as claimed by the classical writers, what is the nature of profit? Let us assume for a moment that capitalists have no other function but "advancing" wages paid to workers. If the price of goods never exceeded their wage costs (or, to put it differently, if the value of any commodity was equal to the value of the amount of hours worked to produce it), how would capitalists be able to make a profit?

Marx's response essentially consisted in taking up the argument that the Physiocrats used regarding land and applying it to labor. According to the Physiocrats, only land has the property of being able to produce "more" than it costs to maintain it. Marx applied this "divine" property to labor—which, he explained, has the unique property of producing more hours than it costs to reproduce it (in terms of its physiological functions). A worker who needs to consume a food product that was made in 4 hours may work 8 hours or more. The gap between the value of the labor force and the value of its output (the number of hours worked) constitutes the surplus value—the concept that is the foundation of Marx's entire economic theory. Because of the competition among workers, they will get paid only what it costs them to get nourished; the capitalist will earn the difference. Competition among capitalists (rather than among workers) would have the opposite effect, but the misery of the workers which was observable in Marx's days would not have made this assumption a realistic one.

What about capital? Capital is the sum total of machines and other equipment which are needed for the manufacturing of goods and which capitalists have to put in the hands of workers. So the value of a commodity is the sum of its manufacturing costs, labor plus capital. But while the value of labor force (what it takes to hire it) is inferior to the product it delivers, capital for its part is like "dead labor"; it can only "give back" what it has cost. In order to determine the capitalist's profit rate, one has to divide the surplus value originating from the sole labor force by the sum of all manufacturing costs: capital and labor. While the numerator is limited by the physiological capacities of the labor force, there is no limit to the denominator's increase. There is a tendency therefore for the profit rate to fall. The contradiction which presides over the fate of capitalism now becomes clear. An enormous accumulation of capital is needed to produce goods, but the basis of profit is more or less constant: it is the labor force. In order to survive, capitalism tries to make workers as poor as possible in absolute (or, at least, in relative) terms, but there must come a point when this ends in a revolution that will close the capitalist era.

Marginalism

According to Marx, capital is "dead labor." Albert Marshall, one of the founders of "Marginalism," writing in the late nineteenth century, takes a somewhat identical point of departure in his analysis. The stock of capital which a society has accumulated is there at every moment, "dead," intangible. While Marx compares capital to crystallized labor, Marginalists regard capital, at a certain point in time, as "land"—not the Physiocrats' generous land, but the classical writers' avaricious land, which cannot be (instantaneously) increased. Given a certain stock of capital, one can try to increase the output by raising the number of workers; however, just like agricultural workers (in classical theory), those workers (in Marshall's theory) are being exposed to the danger of lower productivity. Unless the number of machines available to workers increases proportionately, the law of diminishing returns appears once more. At the "margin," productivity decreases. And at any point in time, capital then gets rewarded for the same reason for which land gets rewarded in Ricardo's analysis: because it earns a rent that corresponds to its relative scarcity.

It is, however, possible to increase capital through saving and thus escape the law of diminishing returns. In this sense capital differs from land: it can be increased over the years. But how far can one go in accumulating capital? While there is no easy quantitative answer, one can say with certainty that the accumulation of capital per worker cannot grow indefinitely. An increasing number of machines per worker would indeed open the back door to the law of diminishing returns. For a given number of workers, the productivity of machines goes down as one keeps increasing their number, for reasons exactly symmetrical to those that cause workers' productivity to go down as one increases the number of those operating on a given stock of machines.

At the level of society at large, it is possible to make capital accumulation go hand in hand with an increase in the number of workers, provided saving takes place. However, capital growth cannot (over a long period of time) keep a faster pace than the increase in the number of workers. So this reasoning, while it differs from Marx's, essentially leads to the same prediction made by Marx: that capitalism cannot tolerate an indefinite increase of capital per capita without making the profit rate go down. The pursuit of capital accumulation, and hence the growth of the economy, must stop sooner or later.

Conclusion

In the second half of the nineteenth century, Marxist and Marginalist theories reaffirmed the same prediction, inspired by classical thought but transposed from the agricultural sector to the industrial sector: the accumulation of capital cannot by itself result in an indefinite growth in wealth. The reason is that it necessarily comes face to face with the law of diminishing returns and interrupts the production of wealth by nations. According to Marginalist writers as well as Marx, growth is only possible in proportion to population growth. This is their only (but obviously significant) concession to "modernity" in relation to the classical writers (who claimed that population cannot exceed a limit set by the available land). But in spite of the extensive transformations they witnessed in their days, none of the brilliant economists of the nineteenth century ever thought that it was possible for a society to grow richer indefinitely.

Appendix B
The History of the Modern State

The eleventh, twelfth, and thirteenth centuries succeeded in bringing a resumption of trade and the restoration of a money economy. This resulted in the demise of medieval economy. The money economy gradually became part of feudal economic relations. The lords wanted to substitute monetary transfers for the *corvée* system, which limited transfers between peasants and their lords to payments in kind.

This introduction of money within the lord-peasant relationship was going to have a parallel development in the relationship between the kings and their vassals. In the Middle Ages every vassal owed a payment in kind to his suzerain. Over a period of 40 days he owed him a certain number of knights who would later—on the 41st day—be relieved of any obligation. With the development of a money economy, it became possible to replace this payment in kind by a payment of money, called *scutage,* as a way to meet one's obligations to one's suzerain. It allowed the gradual establishment of regular armies, thus freeing monarchs of the vicissitudes inherent in the 40-day system.

The introduction of money in the suzerain-vassal relationship and the subsequent possibility for a king to recruit mercenaries were to encourage the emergence of war "specialists" (English longbowmen, Swiss pikemen, Genovese crossbowmen, and so on), which led to the gradual disappearance of feudal war. That type of war would involve a few dozen armored knights who had the exclusive control over "military technology," wore heavy trapping, and were engaged in wars which were soon to be viewed as having limited scope. Feudal war started losing ground, then was pushed into total oblivion by the battles of Crécy (1340), Poitiers (1356), and Azincourt (1415), which demonstrated that (Flemish) pikemen or (English) archers could defeat (French) knights. From then on the history of war shows increasing sophistication of weapons (artillery would bring victory to the French and the Turks), a growing number of armies and wars, and ever-increasing costs. Until the eighteenth century the future nation-states had a simple political economy: on the one hand, a prince, who was always in dire financial circumstances due to the rising cost of wars; on the other hand, the remainder of society (landless peasants, landowners, and the bourgeoisie), which tried to evade government taxation.

The Fiscal Origins of Democracy

"Starting in the thirteenth or fourteenth century, assemblies came into existence in most countries. In spite of their different names (Estates General, Cortes, etc.) they had common features and the same purpose: confronting the financial needs of nation-states." This passage from Gabriel Ardant's *Histoire de l'Impôt* (Fayard, 1971) sheds a fascinating light on the fiscal origins of our democracies.

In order to show that our present-day democratic institutions definitely have fiscal origins, Ardant forcefully remarks that "no government of any Mediterranean city gave rise to a representative system; such a system was not even considered as a possibility by theorists of political science in antiquity." Why did the empires of antiquity—(which) knew something about taxation—not give rise to institutions of the Estates General type? Ardant suggests two possible answers. First of all, sovereigns in antiquity took advantage of the extensive diversity of social and geographical structures to ground their power in a number of militarily or technically strong provinces in order to dominate others. It was a different matter for sovereigns in European monarchies at the end of the Middle Ages: they were facing a feudal society that was "relatively" homogeneous, geographically speaking, and therefore they could not count on military force as the only way to levy the taxes they needed to sustain their own power.

Ardant makes another important remark about the parallel between political evolution in Rome and political evolution in Western Europe in the late Middle Ages. He notes that in Rome "striking against taxation and conscription, or threatening to do so, enabled plebeians to be admitted to high positions in the City. The Roman Republic was forced to grant citizenship to new categories of people in order to be able to recruit armies among Latins, Italians and Provincials. . . . In Western Europe, on the other hand, the evolution of military art in the Middle Ages had given rise to professional armies while artillery, a costly material, was taking on more and more significance; as a result, *the need for money was replacing the need for men.*" It was not until the French Revolution that the conscription of "a nation at arms" reversed the course of events (and revived the issue of citizenship). Before examining it, let us first review how England found its way toward democracy.

The English Revolution

In May of 1214, English barons marched to London to persuade John Lackland to renounce his decision to impose an exceptional scutage (from which only the barons who had gone to France with him were exempt). John had to retreat and approved the Magna Carta, a document that anticipated the French Revolution's Declaration of Human Rights by several centuries. The barons obtained the promise that the king would commit to ensuring impartial justice and guaranteeing individual freedoms. But most important were, at the heart of the text, limitations on the king's power to make fiscal decisions. The barons did not ask to be granted any control over the composition of expenditures (it was not until the fifteenth century that they requested justifications for royal expenses); in the thirteenth century their pressure led the king to agree to seek the approval of the Magnum Concilium for any tax increases.

Why did England's representative institutions resist the rising power of the Crown, unlike their European counterparts?

At the height of monarchy in England, the Tudors attempted to increase their resources by using the same method of selling privileges and grants as the kings of France or Spain, thus favoring existing monopolies (which guaranteed a better fiscal yield for them) and choking the economy. However, two factors were to separate the fate of the monarchy of England from that of France or Spain. The first resulted from the expropriation of the clergy. In order to increase his revenues (and, incidentally, get remarried), Henry VIII appropriated the possessions of the Church. Although this removed some of his budgetary constraints and made it easier for him to obtain Parliament's approval of his expenses, it also weakened his legitimacy (and consequently made the legitimacy of the communes even more necessary). The second factor was also of a fiscal nature: in order to solve her budgetary problems, Queen Elizabeth I financed some lucrative piracy operations; they also made for less tension between her and the Parliament and constituted an alternative to the establishment of a strong bureaucracy capable of collecting taxes.

Since it was always consulted by the Tudors, the English Parliament was able to maintain and reinforce its legitimacy. When the Stuarts attempted to resolve their financial problems, they always had to face a Parliament whose help they needed all the more since the kingdom had not set up an efficient system of fiscal administration. In Ardant's words: "The key to English history lies in the fact that the Crown was unable to increase its tax revenues through efficient control. It could not be done without a large and obedient administrative body, the possibility of really controlling industry through the guilds and—finally—a legislative system subjected to royal authority."

In other words, circumventing their financial problems through piracy and the expropriation of the clergy resulted for the Tudors in leaving central power in the hands of a legitimate institution other than their own: the communes.

Two revolutions, one in 1648 and one in 1688, would nevertheless be needed for an equilibrium to be reached between Parliament and the Crown. In the words of Ardant: "The 13 articles of the 1689 Declaration of Rights, which was really a pact between Parliament and the new monarchs, established not only the Assembly's fiscal power—with the king being forbidden to raise taxes or an army without Parliament's approval—but also its legislative power: the king could not exempt anyone from observing the law. However, the principle of the existence of two powers—the king's and the Assembly's—was retained. . . . The very notion of 'pact,' which was

given philosophical content by Locke, reflected this idea of
co-existence, a natural outcome for this fiscally based constitu-
tional development."

The French Revolution

In 1789, the French monarchy was essentially bankrupt. Its
contribution to the War of Independence in America probably
proved to be the one bridge too far. Management of the treas-
ury was left to the Swiss banker Necker, who rescheduled the
debt at higher and higher interest rates. Rather than default,
the French king Louis XVI decided to require the Estates General to let him proceed with tax reform to save the kingdom's
finance. For the first time since 1614, the Estates General, in
which the aristocrats, the clergy, and the Third Estate (the rest
of society) were represented equally, was convened. In one form
or another, this parliament was never to close its sessions, and
it was eventually to cut off the king's head.

The French Revolution abolished all rights and patents that
the Old Regime had instituted. It declared the abolition of
guilds and corporations, the abolition of the fiscal privileges
granted to the aristocrats over the centuries, and eventually the
expropriation of the aristocrats' lands. We should obviously
not deceive ourselves about the economic rationality presiding
over revolutionary choices. The parcels of land redistributed by
the Revolution were usually too small to allow an efficient
development of agricultural production. The Industrial Revolution—which was starting to take place *before* the Revolution
in France, as historians have shown—was delayed for several
decades *because* of the Revolution. Yet the expropriation of the
clergy and part of the aristocracy (which the post-Napoleonic
restoration of the monarchy could not reverse) enabled peas-

ants to achieve their century-long dream of land ownership.
And once they became landlords, the peasants formed invinci-
ble battalions of defenders of "private property." The "sacred"
respect for private property that was inscribed in the Declaration of Human Rights (at a time when the Revolution decided
to expropriate wealth in an unprecedented way) originates in
this political and economic advancement of the peasantry. The
peasants' blocking of a new redistribution of wealth is at the
root of French political sociology in the nineteenth century. As
this influence loosened over the century, the challenge to private
property reappeared: socialist ideas and the call for an income
tax moved forward.

Obviously the political scene, even more than the economic
scene, was radically changed by the French Revolution, which
invented the "sovereign nation," the new equation that was to
preside over the political economic problem of nation-states
during the nineteenth century. The French Revolution put "the
nation at arms" and by so doing radically changed the way in
which later wars were to be fought—and consequently the way
in which nation-states had to handle their fiscal problems.
Indeed, warring monarchies needed money rather than men
once nation-states had to decide (from the fourteenth century
on) to use mercenaries to build up permanent armies. In order
to counter the assaults of the monarchies that were attacking
it, the Revolution mobilized a "nation at arms," which provided gigantic armies out of proportion to those that could be
mobilized by the enemy forces. As a result of this conscription
of a people, nation-states could no longer lend a deaf ear to the
"national" aspirations that were to set fire to Europe during
the nineteenth century. No army of mercenaries can measure
up to a nation at arms. The same intra-European rivalry that
had pushed nation-states to the limits of their solvency was to

spread revolutions, and eventually democracies, all over Europe. But it was the English who invented, with the income tax, the means by which these democracies were eventually given a content.

The Income Tax

In England the history of the income tax began as early as the time of the French Revolution. Just before the war against France, the British budget relied essentially on customs duties and domestic consumption. At the beginning of the war, "Old Regime" taxes—taxes on hair powder, dogs, watches, clocks, etc.—were gradually raised. William Pitt promptly realized that a "nation at arms" could not be vanquished with such expedients. Taxpayers were then divided into three classes: those who owned a carriage and male servants (class 1), those who owned houses, watches, and clocks (class 2), and all other taxpayers (class 3). Each class paid the previous year's amount of taxes plus a coefficient which increased in proportion to those taxes. This tax system, which Pitt's political opponents would call "Robespierre's child," was voted in on January 12, 1798. But the income tax was an instrument at the service of a foreign war, not an instrument of redistribution. It was abolished as soon as the war against Napoleon ended.

But the harm had been done. The income tax reappeared as early as 1842. Sir Robert Peel calculated that lower customs duties (on wheat) resulted in less misery for the people (who were quite miserable during the "hungry forties") and could be offset by restoring the income tax. The 1806 tax was restored by a 1842 law and has been a British institution ever since.

Income taxes were instituted in Sweden (1861), Italy (1864), Japan (1867), Saxony (1874), and various German states (1891 to 1903). In the United States, after a first attempt in 1862 (during the Civil War) failed, an income tax was instituted in 1894. The Supreme Court found it to be unconstitutional, but the Constitution was amended and the income tax was permanently established in 1913. In France, Joseph Caillaux obtained a vote in favor of the income tax in 1914 in spite of the Senate's opposition.

The difference between England and other countries in this respect should be noted. On the eve of World War I, England's House of Lords tried to block progressive taxes, which it regarded as contradictory to the notion of equality before the law. This was to be that house's last political battle, and its defeat took away all its political power. In Prussia the debate on progressive taxes started in 1891. However, Bismarck's Germany was to go further. Medical insurance was instituted in 1883, and the social history of the twentieth century began.

Appendix C
Underconsumption Theories

Is it possible for growth to be interrupted for lack of outlets? Malthus thought so, as is evident from Keynes's statement that "the principle of saving, pushed to excess, would destroy the motive to production." Ricardo, faithful to the tradition initiated by J. B. Say, thought the opposite.

Let us briefly return to Malthus's demonstration. If all income were in the hands of the bourgeoisie, one of two things would have to happen: either the bourgeoisie would "hoard" its wealth and the demand for commodities would be too weak, or it would reinvest its wealth, in which case the demand for equipment goods would provide outlets for the output for a while, but the problem would later reappear on a broader basis. By reinvesting its income, the bourgeoisie increases the productive capacity of an economy without increasing its aggregate spending capacity. If one believes that the time will necessarily come when supply will have expanded to such an extent that the bourgeoisie will hesitate to reinvest its income, then a serious overproduction crisis will necessarily be triggered.

Ricardo's answer to Malthus was fairly dogmatic. It goes as follows: For a capitalist, the act of saving is either the act of investing or (if he is hoarding) the purchase of gold. But gold is a commodity like any other. It is produced in mines, it is bought, and it is sold. If capitalists decided to keep their wealth in the form of money, they would open a new market for mine products. (The fact that gold must be "imported," rather than produced domestically, does not modify the sense of this demonstration: "importing" gold means "selling" goods in exchange for gold imported from abroad.) This demonstration may be "technically" right, but historically speaking it is somewhat unsatisfactory.

The debate between Malthus and Ricardo is limited by the absence of a convincing theory of consumption. Being mostly concerned with the theory of supply, the classical writers left the theory of consumption as they had found it in previous theories: workers eat, capitalists accumulate, landowners spend. This is the categorization that Malthus extrapolated. If workers consume only agricultural products and landowners disappear, the capitalist machine turns into an indefinite accumulation of wealth which nobody will ever consume. It is not illogical to conclude that accumulation will stop one day for a lack of outlets.

A number of authors have made efforts to build a theory of demand. Léon Walras stands out for most clearly and lucidly attempting to understand the overall functioning of market processes. Today his theory of "general equilibrium" is regarded as the foundation of "neoclassical" theory. This theory, which "demonstrates" the impossibility of overproduction crises, was to be implicitly fought by Keynes.

The simplest way to approach the theory of general equilibrium is to go straight to the central issue: Can there be crises of *general* overproduction? Can supply exceed demand on *all* markets? It is important to stress the words "on all markets": Producers can be "mistaken" about the demand and produce more than is necessary in some markets, but can they be mistaken about all markets at once? Neoclassical theory answered this question in the negative; Keynes countered with a positive answer. Walras considered the total set of markets that organize the economy of a society; he called a situation in which the supply induced by this price system is exactly equal to the demand in every market a "general equilibrium."

Can there be "general overproduction"? That is, can the supply induced by a price system (whatever it might be) exceed the demand in every market? In Walras's system the answer has to be negative. Walras's demonstration is simple: Insofar as agents necessarily distribute the *total amount* of their income over the whole set of markets, and insofar as their income is derived from the output of the firms themselves, the sum of expenditures is equal to total output (which is equal to the total income). If a disequilibrium is present in one market, there will necessarily be an opposing disequilibrium in another market. If a firm produces "too many" potatoes relative to the demand (induced by prices), it necessarily means that, say, cauliflower producers are producing *too few* cauliflowers.

The key to Walras's demonstration in this regard is that agents spend the total amount of their income. This does not mean that agents do not save or hoard. As Ricardo pointed out to Malthus, if agents hoard it simply means that they want gold—which is a commodity like any other. If they save, it means that they are buying securities. Let us now set aside the problem of government. If agents want to save, it means that they *buy* claims on firms. In Walras's system such claims on firms are commodities like any other. When Walras explains that agents spend the whole amount of their income, he is using the term in a tautological sense, as Ricardo did. Income not "spent" on an ordinary commodity is income "spent" on gold or securities. Thus, it is possible that an excess supply of ordinary commodities can exist; but it means that agents want claims on firms, that is, more firms—which means more investments. At the equilibrium point, firms will have to reduce the supply of ordinary commodities and invest (by using the resources which agents want to make available to them on the securities market), and thus increase the production of future commodities.

It all seems so simple that one could almost forget that capitalism is so often plagued with unemployment and financial crises. The 1929 crisis acted as a reminder. Keynes won the race for an explanation. His critique can easily be expressed within Walras's system. A jobless individual does not get any income, so he cannot spend it. By contrast, Walras implicitly assumes that a jobless individual continues to consume "as if" his income corresponded to his expectations. In modern terms one would say "as if he expected his unemployment to be temporary enough for him not to have to reduce his demand." As soon as the unemployed individual adjusts his expenses to his actual income, the vicious circle evoked by Keynes may appear: lower income results in lower spending and consequently fewer outlets for firms, which results in less hiring, and so on. This leads to an equilibrium in which firms do not hire the unemployed because the unemployed cannot spend what they would earn if they were unemployed. Why the unemployed would not underbid the salaries of the employed (however inefficient this might be socially) is the one question that modern theories of unemployment (reviewed in chapter 2) have attempted to address.

Notes

Chapter 1

1. Jean Fourastié, *Les Trent Glorieuses* (Fayard, 1979).

2. Ibid., p. 31.

3. The story of this section is told in more detail in appendix A.

4. Nicholas Kaldor, "Capital accumulation and economic growth," in *The Theory of Capital,* ed. F. A. Lutz and D. C. Hague (St. Martin's, 1961).

5. Here we will follow Paul Romer's discussion of these facts. See Romer's "Capital accumulation in the theory of long run growth," in *Modern Business Cycle Theory,* ed. R. Barro (Harvard University Press, 1991).

6. Robert Solow, "A contribution to the theory of economic growth," *Quarterly Journal of Economics* 70 (1956): 65–94.

7. Angus Maddison, *Dynamic Forces in Capitalist Development* (Oxford University Press, 1991), table 5.19.

8. Paul Romer, "Increasing returns and long run growth," in *Equilibrium Theory and Amplifications: Proceedings of the Sixth International Symposium in Economic Theory and Econometrics* (Cambridge University Press, 1991). Romer's major works are "Crazy explanations for the productivity slowdown" (in *NBER Macroeconomics Annual 1987*), "Capital accumulation in the theory of long run growth" (note 4 above), and "Increasing returns and long run growth" (*Journal of Political Economy* 94 (1986): 1002–1037. The other founding article is Robert Lucas's "On the mechanics of economic

development" (*Journal of Monetary Economics,* July 1988: 3–42). Robert Barro's "Economic growth in a cross-section of country" (*Quarterly Journal of Economics,* May 1992), which has greatly modified the empirical approach to problems of growth, should also be mentioned.

9. Adam Smith, *An Inquiry into the Nature and Causes of the Wealth of Nations* (first edition: 1776).

10. Joseph Schumpeter, *Capitalism, Socialism and Democracy* (first edition: 1942). The renewal of Schumpeterian theories is best illustrated by Philippe Aghion and Peter Howitt's paper "A model of growth through creative destruction" (*Econometrica* 2 (1992): 323–351).

11. Paul Bairoch, "*Le tiers-monde dans l'impasse* (Gallimard, 1971; second edition 1983), p. 101ff.

12. Fourastié, *Les Trent Glorieuses,* p 106.

13. On this point, and for a critique of other standard explanations, see Alwyn Young, "Lessons from East Asian NICs: A contrarian view," *European Economic Review (Papers and Proceedings)* 38 (1994): 954–973.

14. Paul Krugman, *The Age of Diminished Expectations* (MIT Press, 1990).

Chapter 2

1. Alfred Sauvy, *La machine et le chômage* (Dunod, 1980).

2. Montesquieu, quoted in Sauvy, *La machine et le chômage* (ibid.).

3. Sismonde de Sismondi, *Nouveaux principes d'économie politique, ou de la richesse dans ses rapports à la population* (quoted by A. Sauvy, ibid., p. 55).

4. Ibid.

5. D. Cohen and G. Saint-Paul develop these ideas in Uneven Technical Progress and Job Destructions (CEPREMAP working paper 9412).

6. William Baumol, Sue Anne Batey Blackman, and Edward N. Wolf, *Productivity and American Leadership: The Long View* (MIT Press, 1989).

7. Ibid.

8. Christopher Pissarides, *Equilibrium Unemployment Theory* (Blackwell, 1990).

9. Michael Emerson, *What Model for Europe?* (MIT Press, 1988); Michael Burda, "Is mismatch really the problem?" in *Europe's Unemployment Problem,* ed. J. H. Drèze and C. R. Bean (MIT Press, 1991).

10. Nicholas Kiefer and George P. Neuman, *Search Models and Applied Labour Economics* (Cambridge University Press, 1989).

11. Michael Bruno and Jeffrey Sachs, *The Economics of Worldwide Stagnation* (Harvard University Press, 1985).

12. Lars Calmfors and John Driffill, "Bargaining structure, Corporatism and macroeconomic performance," *Economic Policy* 11 (1988): 13–61.

13. Assar Lindbeck and Dennis Snower, *The Insider-Outsider theory of Unemployment* (MIT Press, 1989). See also Olivier Blanchard and Larry Summers, "Hysteresis and the European unemployment problem," in *NBER Macroeconomics Annual 1986.*

14. Steve Davis, "Cross country patterns of change in relative wages," in *NBER Macroeconomics Annual 1992.*

15. Olivier Blanchard and Peter Diamond, "Ranking, unemployment, duration and wages," *Review of Economic Studies* 61 (1994): 417–434.

16. Angus Maddison, *Dynamic Forces in Capitalist Development* (Oxford University Press, 1991), p. 159.

17. Philippe Séguin, *Ce que j'ai dit* (Grasset, 1993).

Chapter 3

1. See appendix B for more details.

2. In *Essays in Persuasion,* published by Keynes in the 1920s and reprinted by Norton in 1963. See p. 68.

3. Ibid., p. 244.

4. Ibid., p. 90.

5. See appendix C for more details.

6. See appendix C.

7. Quoted on p. 27 of Béatrice Majmoni d'Intignano's book *La protection sociale* (Fallois, 1993).

8. Christine André and Robert Delorme, "Matériaux pour une comparaison internationale des dépenses publiques en longue période. Le cas de six pays industrialisés," in *Statistiques et Etudes Financières* (Ministère de l'Economie et des Finances, 1983). (Their data are presented in an appendix to the present chapter.)

9. See appendix B.

10. Robert Delorme and Christine André, *L'Etat et l'économie* (Editions du Seuil, 1983).

11. They are quoted in Aaron's survey "Economic aspects of the role of government in health care," in *Health, Economics and Health Economics,* ed. J. van der Gaag and M. Perlman (North-Holland, 1981).

12. Paul Samuelson, "An exact consumption loan model with or without the social contrivance of money," *Journal of Political Economy* 68 (1958) 467–487.

13. Maurice Allais, *Economie et intérêt* (Imprimerie Nationale, 1947).

Chapter 4

1. Milton Friedman, "The role of monetary policy," *American Economic Review* 58 (1968): 1–17.

2. Robert E. Lucas, Jr., *Studies in Business-Cycle Theory* (MIT Press, 1991).

3. Fynn Kydland and Robert Prescott, "Rules rather than discretion," *Journal of Political Economy* 85 (1977): 473–491.

4. For more details see Daniel Cohen, *Private Lending to Sovereign States* (MIT Press, 1991).

5. See Barry Eichengreen and Robert Lindert, *The Developing Debt Crisis in Historical Perspective* (MIT Press, 1988).

6. For more details see C. Bean, D. Cohen, F. Giavazzi, J. von Hagen, D. Neven, X. Vives, and C. Wyplosz, "L'Union Monétaire face à ses critiques," *Le Monde* no. 14764, July 1992.

7. Olivier Blanchard and Larry Katz, Brookings Papers on Economic Activity no. 1, 1992.

Chapter 5

1. The classic in this area is Anthony Downs, *An Economic Theory of Democracy* (Harper, 1957). This section is based on D. Cohen, "What caused the rise of conservatism?" *Economic Policy* 6 (1988): 198–212.

2. See, for example, Douglas Hibbs, *The Political Economy of Industrial Democracies* (Harvard University Press, 1987), and Alberto Alesina, "Macroeconomics and politics," in *NBER Macroeconomics Annual 1988*.

3. Kenneth Rogoff and Anne Sibert, "Elections and Macroeconomic Policy Cycles," *Review of Economic Studies* 55 (1988), no.181: 1–16.

4. Alberto Alesina, "Macroeconomics and politics," in *NBER Macroeconomics Annual 1988*.

5. D. Kondratieff, "The long waves in economic life" (translated. from the Russian in 1925), reprinted in *The Long Wave Cycle,* ed. J. M. Snyder (Richardson and Snyder, 1984).

6. Gaston Imbert, *Des mouvements de longue durée Kondratiev* (La Pensée Universitaire, 1959).

7. Ibid.

8. Ibid.

9. In this respect the lesson we can draw from a comparison of electricity and computers is promising: it is only after World War I that electricity became a mass consumption good. See Paul David, "The computer and the dynamo: An historical perspective on the modern productivity paradox," *American Economic Review,* May 1990: 355–361.

10. Alvin Hansen, *Economic Stabilization in an Unbalanced World* (Harcourt, Brace, 1932).

11. Alec L. Macfie, "The outbreak of war and the trace cycle," Economic History (addendum to *Economic Journal*), February 1958.

12. Paul Kennedy, *The Rise and Fall of the Great Powers* (Random House, 1987).

13. Karl Polanyi, *The Great Transformation: The Political And Economic Origins of Our Time* (Beacon, 1957; first edition 1944).

14. Albert Hirshman, *Shifting Involvements, Private Interest and Public Action* (Princeton University Press, 1982).

15. Marcel Proust, *A la recherche du temps perdu,* volume 3 (Gallimard).

Appendix A

1. Henri Mendras, *The Vanishing Peasant: Innovation and Change in French Agriculture* (MIT Press, 1971).

2. For the general area covered in this appendix, see Douglas North and Robert Thomas, *The Rise of the Western World: A New Economic History* (Cambridge University Press, 1973).

3. Paul Bairoch, *Le Tiers-monde dans l'impasse* (Gallimard, 1971; second (expanded) edition 1983). Soboul's quotation is also taken from this book.

4. Jean-Claude Asselain, *Histoire économique de la France,* volume 1 (Le Seuil).

5. François Quesnay, *Maximes générales du gouvernement économique d'un royaume agricole* (1758) and *Tableau économique des physiocrates* (reprinted by Calmann-Lévy, 1969).

6. Ibid.

7. Many introductory books on economic thought provide a good introduction to the issues discussed here. See, e.g., J. A. Schumpeter, *History of Economic Analysis* (Allen and Unwin, 1954); K. Pribram, *A History of Economic Reasoning* (Johns Hopkins University Press, 1983).

Index